Valuing Sexuality
A Guide For Catholic Teens

Richard D. Parsons

BROWN-ROA
A Division of Harcourt Brace & Company

Dubuque, Iowa

Book Team

Publisher—Ernest T. Nedder
Editorial Director—Sandra Hirstein
Production Editor—Karla A. McCarey
Production Manager—Marilyn Rothenberger
Art Director—Cathy Frantz
Illustrator—Rob Suggs

ISBN 0–697–02532–2

21 22 23 24 25 26 27 28 29 30

Contents

Preface v

Chapter 1:   Made in God's Image 1

Chapter 2:   Valuing Values 11

Chapter 3:   Male and Female: God
Created Them 23

Chapter 4:   Feelings of Attraction 35

Chapter 5:   Equality of Males and
Females 47

Chapter 6:   Making Decisions 55

Chapter 7:   Developing Relationships 69

Chapter 8:   Saying No 79

Chapter 9:   New Human Life 89

Chapter 10: Making the Heart Grow
Fonder 97

Chapter 11: It Takes Two 103

Chapter 12: There Is No Easy Answer 113

Chapter 13: Staying Healthy 123

Chapter 14: Some Touch Hurts 133

Chapter 15: Being an Askable Parent
(or Friend) 143

Dedication

For Robert McKay Brooks, O.Praem, a man who valued life, social justice, faith, and his fellow pilgrims.

Preface

For all too long, the topic of sex and sexuality has been narrowly defined and often cloaked in secrecy. Sexuality involves much more than male or female genitals and much more than what happens between two individuals in the privacy of their bedroom.

Sexuality is a total human experience. It is a gift of your creation. It is to be enjoyed, to be valued and prized. But, like all gifts, your sexuality is to be handled responsibly and maturely. Learning to value, enjoy, and *responsibly* handle your own sexuality is one of the very special and often most difficult tasks of the teen years.

Adolescence

The teen years are a time of unique feelings and sensations. It is a time when the "old" of childhood gives way to the "new" of the emerging adult. Adolescence is a time of many new gifts, many new opportunities, many new experiences, and many new decisions. Adolescence is a very special time of change.

A Time of Change

With the beginning of adolescence a number of physical, psychological, and social changes begin to occur. These changes are often scary, even uncomfortable and outright painful.

The changes in how you look, what you feel, how you think and what those around you demand of you, often seem overwhelming. There are times when you might just wish that you had never left childhood.

There may be times when you feel like you simply don't know what's happening or what will happen. You may feel confused by all of the unanswered questions and the many decisions which you need to make. But as you learn to cope with the new situations you face, you will come to know more fully the wonder and beauty of God's most valued creation—you!

In the book entitled *The Little Prince*, a fragile little rose speaks to its very protective prince about the struggles and pain of life: "In life one must experience two or three caterpillars if one is to know the butterflies."

Adolescence is filled with many caterpillars. It is certainly a period of storm and stress. But just as the prince was warned of the need to experience the caterpillars in order to know the beauty of the butterfly, you must be mindful that the storm and stress of adolescence is necessary if you are to know the wonders of your emerging identity and the special plan God holds in store for you.

A Time of Transformation

The tasks of adolescence are many. During your teen years, you are required to:

- Break away from your childhood dependencies
- Develop more mature social relationships with your peers, parents, and other adults
- Become comfortable with your own body and your sexuality
- Prepare for vocational and occupational futures

These tasks serve as the foundation or basis for the "business" or work of the teenage years.

Perhaps more important than any of these tasks is the fact that, over the course of the next few years, you will begin to re-assess your beliefs, your attitudes, your values. You will need to develop a system of values and ideals which will guide you in all of your actions and decisions.

It is in the hope of assisting you with that developing system of values that this book was written. Even though much of the discussion centers on the issue of sex and your developing sexuality, the goal of the book is much broader than simply discussing your biological and social-sexual changes. The purpose of this text is to assist you in understanding your sexuality within the context of your adolescent experience.

Throughout the text, adolescence is presented as a time of decision. The choices you have and the decisions you are asked to make are many. Each decision you make may take you down special paths or pull you from other equally wonderful paths. There are so many different paths, and they all look so enticing.

While there are many variables and many different decisions, the one constant throughout it all is God. Regardless of which paths you select, and regardless of which decisions you make, your constant companion will be the Lord. Like the disciples as they walked the road to Emmaus, you may not recognize the Lord as He walks beside you, but whether you recognize Him or not, He is with you.

The question which you and I and all Christians need to continually ask ourselves, in our joys and in our sorrows is: "Where is the Lord in this situation, and what is He asking of me?"

A Wonderful Time

It may be hard to believe, especially if you just broke up with a boyfriend or girlfriend, or if your parents seem unbearable, or if school is becoming intolerable, **but** these teen years are wonderful years.

My hope is that as you continue to grow and learn, you will more fully appreciate and enjoy the wonder of these teen years. Moreover, I hope that the new knowledge and skills you are gaining will enable you to see each new experience, each new decision, each new opportunity as invitations by Christ to ". . . Come, follow me." (Mark 10:21)

Chapter 1
Made in God's Image

God said: "Let us make man in our own image, in the likeness of ourselves, and let them be masters of the fish of the sea, the birds of heaven, the cattle, all the wild animals and all the creatures that creep along the ground." God created man in the image of himself, in the image of God he created him, male and female he created them.
—Genesis 1:26–27

It is hard sometimes for us to remember that God did create us in His image. When we look around the world and find so much pain and injustice, we may question how a world and a people who act like this could be made in the image of God.

Even with all of the less than God-like things that exist in the world, and even when we feel less than good or attractive, the truth remains that we **are** created in His image. We are created as a reflection of His love and given our own potential to love and to grow in His love.

Responding to God's invitation to grow in His love and learning to accept ourselves and each other in love—these are the major tasks awaiting you as you enter your teen years.

The Teen Years

Cracking voices, erupting skin, fuzzy chins, and budding breasts may all be announcements that you are in the process of transforming from a child to an adult, but these announcements certainly can come at times and in ways that cause you much embarrassment. These physical happenings, which you experience during the early stages of your adolescence, are not only announcements that your body is changing and maturing, but they also announce that *you* are changing! Your sense of who you are (your self-concept), is being revised.

Adolescence brings with it so many changes and so many new demands that many teenagers find that their sense of personal value, their self-esteem may be threatened. You may worry that others won't like you, or that you won't fit in, or that you won't make the team.

The changes in your body may have put you at a different place than the other people in your class. Maybe you haven't started to show the same degree of physical development as your classmates. Or, you may have begun to mature much earlier than anyone else in your class. It is hard to feel secure and good about yourself when you seem to look so weird, so different from everyone else! And yet, through it all, you are still a reflection of God's love, and made in God's image.

Self-Concept

The term *self-concept* refers to a set of ideas you have about yourself which help you know who you are and what makes you different from everyone and everything else. The development of a self-concept is an ongoing process.

When you were eight, you may have found it easy to answer the question: "Who are you?" You may have stated your name, sex, age, likes, and dislikes and maybe even listed your talents or aspirations. All these different points are references to who you are. At eight years old, it is easy to answer the question of identity by stating: "I am Rick. I am a boy. My best friend is Denis. I like to play football and basketball. I don't like girls. I'm great at computer games and someday I am going to be a pro-basketball player. I am smart."

Throughout the early school years, your experiences help you become more or less confirmed in this self-concept, this identity. For example, making the school's basketball team, or having your friends tell you how good you are, or getting a dollar from your grandparents because of a good report card—all reinforce and strengthen that self-concept, that identity of being a scholar, athlete, and good friend!

As you enter adolescence, you may still answer the question of who you are by stating your name, sex, age, and even likes and dislikes. However, as you move into your teen years, you begin to realize that these responses just don't seem to answer the question completely. Somehow, trying to answer a question as important as "Who are you?" by simply stating your name, sex, or age, just doesn't seem sufficient anymore! Things that once seemed simple now seem much more complex and involved. You are aware that being a boy or a girl, a male or a female, is much more than simply a matter of anatomy. You have many thoughts, many perspectives, and many possibilities. The almost endless options of what you can do, can become, can be, make a simple answer to the question of identity impossible. It can be very confusing and even quite scary.

I remember one young friend of mine, whom we'll call Jacob although that's not his real name. Jacob shared a dream that he had. The dream not only demonstrates the many changes of adolescence but also reflects how frightening these changes can be.

Jacob said: "I had a dream. . . no, not a dream. . . a nightmare. I saw myself waking up and found myself in someone else's body. It was unrecognizable. It was as if I were trapped in some type of shell. There were internal feelings and sensations which were occurring which were alien to me. The body seemed to change hourly and I had no control over it. I didn't even have a sense of its direction or the ultimate outcome. It was as if I had absolutely no control!

"My friends and family—they all changed. Not physically, but the way they treated me, the way they looked at me. They changed all the rules. Sometimes I had to do this or that and other times I was forbidden from doing those very same things. There didn't seem to be any rhyme or reason for the rules imposed on me. I felt like a victim in a strange world and with no control.

"But the scariest thing of all was that even those things that I valued, that I cherished, that seemed to be so much a natural part of who I was, began to change. I felt differently about my family, the rules of society, religion, rights, and wrongs. Everything needed to be re-examined.

"It was as if I were someone else, but I had no idea who! I didn't know who I was or where I was going or what was important anymore. I wanted to scream, to run, to just **escape!**"

Most persons your age share the concerns that surfaced in Jacob's dream. The many changes confronting each of you as

3

you enter and go through your teen years often challenge your ideas about who you are, your self-concept. Your changing bodies, the new social groups in which you find yourself, the new thoughts and changing beliefs you begin to develop, your questioning of previously held rules and values are all part of the adolescent experience. They are all quite threatening to your sense of identity.

Self-Esteem: My Valuing of Me

In addition to the changes in the way you see yourself (your self-concept), there comes a change in the way you evaluate yourself (your self-esteem). For example, you may see yourself as a fifteen-year-old female (part of your self-concept), but you may feel that you are unattractive and undesirable (part of your self-evaluation or self-esteem).

Self-esteem develops as a result of how you have experienced your personality, your "self," as you interact with your environment. For example, persons who experience a high degree of success throughout elementary school (good student, most popular or prettiest eighth grader, captain of the safety squad, star athlete, and so on) most likely see themselves quite positively and have high self-esteem. However, when these same individuals begin thinking that they are no longer the best looking or the funniest or the brightest or the most athletic, then their positive view of themselves may slip. This certainly was the case for Denise.

Denise is a fifteen-year-old girl who recently moved to a new neighborhood and school. Coming from another region of the United States, Denise spoke with an accent, and she wasn't really sure of what was "in" or what was "out" at her new school.

Initially, the kids were polite to her. But soon, they started making fun of her different style of clothing. They would tease her about the funny way she spoke or the names she used for certain things.

Because Denise's previous school used different textbooks and course materials, she experienced a great many problems adjusting to the demands of her new school. Her grades, which previously were quite good, began to fall drastically.

4

Denise started to hate her new home. She hated her school, but most importantly she hated herself. She couldn't stand the way she sounded, looked, or acted. She was too different from the other kids in the school and she hated it, hated herself.

She started to stay in and not try to make new friends. After all, it was much too painful. Eventually, life was too painful. Feeling so hopeless and so negative about herself, Denise attempted suicide.

Happily, Denise's attempt failed. She was able to get the help she needed in order to feel better about herself and to continue being a happy and productive person.

The Power of Self-Esteem

As evidenced in the story of Denise, your self-esteem is a powerful determinant of how you will act in relation to yourself and to your world.

For example, individuals with high self-esteem are reported to be:

- Self-confident

- Able to take criticism

- Assertive (able to stick up for their rights without violating another's rights)

- Problem solvers with an ability to compromise

- Sensitive, respectful listeners

- Successful and able to approach each new situation with an expectation of success

Whereas, individuals with low self-esteem are reported to be:

- Unrealistic in their evaluation of themselves
  Often these individuals have an overly negative or low evaluation of themselves, or an unrealistic, inflated positive image.

- Inhibited by anxiety
  Low self-esteem makes you pull away from new challenges, new experiences. Your responses to new

demands are often prevented or inhibited because of fear and expectation of failure.

- Rejected by peers
  Because of low self-esteem, these individuals often develop negative, attention-getting behaviors. They may act in extreme ways or dress in ways which draw attention to themselves. They approach others expecting rejection and most often get what they expect.

- Failures
  Individuals with low self-esteem believe they will fail and, therefore, often do.

Since your sense of personal worth or value (self-esteem) is so influential on the way you function, it is important that you understand what influences your self-esteem.

Factors Influencing Self-Esteem

There are four general factors which influence the development of positive self-esteem. These factors are *competence, power, virtue,* and *significance.*

Competence

Competence refers to a person's ability to successfully perform tasks which he or she considers to be important. Competence is a prime ingredient for developing a positive self-esteem.

I am sure you can remember times when you succeeded at a task which you valued. Whether you proved successful in making a team, learning to play an instrument, getting a good grade, lifting a heavier weight, or being accepted by a new group or club, the experience told you that you were competent. It made you feel good about yourself (self-esteem).

Typically, success builds self-esteem, while failure tears it down. When you feel less competent you tend to avoid taking on new challenges or new tasks. Or, you may approach the tasks fearfully expecting that you will most likely fail and, thus, you do fail as predicted. After that, you may start to see yourself as less than competent, less than valuable. You may have a low self-esteem.

Power

A second factor which can influence our self-esteem is *power*. Power refers to the extent to which you feel you can influence your own and others' lives.

This kind of power isn't the same thing as physical strength or force. For example, an auto mechanic has power over me when it comes to fixing my car. If the mechanic, with his or her specialized knowledge, tells me that the tapping sound I hear means I have to have the valves in my car's engine adjusted, I will tend to be influenced by his or her expertise, by his or her "power." Similarly, when you are given opportunities to make decisions that affect your life, even decisions about what clothes to buy, where to go on vacation, what time to come in at night, or when to do your chores, you experience a sense of freedom and independence which helps you feel powerful.

Adolescence is an important period for experiencing the power which comes with increasing skills (expertise) and freedom to make your own decisions (autonomy).

Research has demonstrated that teens with high self-esteem come from families where they have been allowed autonomy or freedom. But this freedom was within well-prescribed limits of clear and fair rules. Therefore, these teens are able to experience the power to make decisions, but within limits or guidelines which insure their success (competency).

Virtue

The third factor which appears to influence your sense of worth (self-esteem), is the degree to which you see yourself as having *virtue*. Virtue refers to an individual's determination to act out of a strong set of moral and ethical standards. While one sometimes falls short of these standards, one continues to strive to behave along the lines prescribed by ethical values.

Individuals who see themselves as having virtue know whether what they do is right or wrong. This knowledge enables them to value themselves even when they fail to live up to their own moral standards.

Significance

The final factor influencing your sense of self-esteem is your sense of *significance*. Significance is the feeling or the perception that you are loved. It is the sense of being approved of, especially by people who are important to you. Significance is a perception which develops from day one. The infant who receives love and support from his or her family will soon come to feel significant.

It is very important to remember that your sense of significance is rooted in your belief as to why others value or love you. For example, maybe you have been told that you are good or bad, depending on what you do. Your value, your worth, is good if you do well in school or share your toys or obey your parents or have friends or even look pretty. Soon you may begin to believe that you have value only if you do or have these things. You see your value as conditional, based on something you *do* or *have* rather than on who you *are*.

That was the case with Denise. Her personal worth was tied to getting good grades, having friends, and dressing a certain way. When these things started to sour, so did her view and value of herself!

While it certainly makes sense to value certain behaviors more than others, the mistake often made is that a person may equate their value as a person with one aspect of their behavior. You need to remember that you are much, much more than how you look or what your grades are or the types of clothes you wear or any other such condition! You are a unique person in your very being. You are valuable because you are you—a unique creation of God.

Christ as Model

We have no better teacher on this matter than Jesus Christ. He reached out and touched those with leprosy; he ate and drank with public sinners; he called to be his friends all who came to him, regardless of what they had or what they did.

Christ was able to view all people as worthwhile, as significant, regardless of their condition. He loved the poor, the less-educated, the sick, as much as he loved the rich, the scholarly, and the healthy.

Our Value Is Insured!

When you question your own value or worthwhileness, or when you feel like you desperately need to win somebody's approval, then you need to stop and really try to understand the meaning, the implications, of the fact that you are a unique creation of God, formed in God's image and likeness—a creation so valuable that God would have His only Son, Jesus, die for you!

You need to really take time to reflect on this message, to attempt to fully comprehend what this says about you. As you come to fully appreciate what this means, you will realize just how awesome it is and how awesome you are because of it!

There is a young girl in our community who recently had to undergo a very serious operation. Because of the length and type of operation, she required an extensive amount of blood. The parish asked for volunteers to contribute blood for use during her operation. Dozens of people turned out and gave blood for her.

Many of the people who volunteered didn't even know the little girl. They didn't care how pretty she was or how well she did in school or if she had designer clothes or anything else. What they knew was that there was a fellow human being who was in trouble. They valued this human being, this little girl, so much that they were willing to give a part of themselves (their blood) for her.

Most of us would feel deeply valued, deeply significant if our community would respond to our needs this way. Well, if you could imagine feeling valued if you were the little girl, how valued you would feel, if you could really understand that GOD, Christ, humbled himself to become a human being, and *die*, with much abuse and much pain, giving *his total being* to *save your life*. Christ didn't care about your designer clothes, your neat hair, your skin color, your brains, or any other such condition. He simply loved you, *unconditionally!*

When I think about how special I make myself feel because another person tells me I am okay, I want to laugh and remind myself that I am more than okay. I am so important that God's only Son would give his life for me. The same is true about you!

In the Image of God

Valuing yourself for who you are and what you are called to be is the basis for a healthy life. Valuing yourself is a reflection of the value and love God holds for you. Valuing yourself reflects God's valuing of you. Valuing yourself is the first step on the road to loving others.

"Love your neighbor as yourself!" (Matthew 19:19) Not *more* than, or *less* than, but *as* yourself.

As you read through this book, you will find help for better understanding who you are and who God is calling you to become. You will come to realize that you have your own special gifts, your own special talents, and your own special crosses to bear.

Valuing yourself will help you value others. Respecting yourself will help you interact with others in respectful ways. Valuing and respecting yourself is the foundation for relationships which are genuine, open, and nonexploitative. Valuing and respecting yourself and others reflects the truth that *we are made in God's image!*

For Reflection and Discussion

- Why is every human being entitled to respect and dignity?

- How has your self-concept changed over the past few years?

- Can you give an example of how each of the following factors can affect self-esteem: competence, power, virtue, and significance?

- What are the things that most affect the way you feel about yourself?

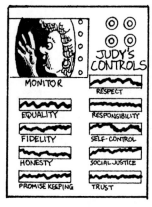

Chapter 2
Valuing
Values

*Since you have been brought back to true life with
Christ, you must look for the things that are in
heaven, where Christ is, sitting at God's right hand.
You are God's chosen race, his saints; he loves you,
and you should be clothed in sincere compassion, in
kindness and humility, gentleness and patience. Bear
with one another; forgive each other as soon as a
quarrel begins. The Lord has forgiven you; now you
must do the same. Over all these clothes, to keep
them together and complete them, put on love.*
—Colossians 3:1, 12–14

As you journey through the many decisions of your teen
years, you will consider a variety of important issues. You will
need to decide about careers, future schooling, vocations,
friends, and family. There will be much to consider and much
to choose. In your choosing, you must, as St. Paul tells us in
his letter to the Colossians, *". . . look for the things that are in
heaven."* (Colossians 3:1)

Your decisions will be guided by your values. Values such
as compassion, humility, kindness, gentleness, patience, and
love will guide you in the direction of the Lord. These are
values to be valued.

Values

What are values? Values are strongly held beliefs which
enable you to make decisions about what is important in your
life. For example, let's say that Dan values honesty in
relationships. When Susan, his girlfriend, asks him why he
didn't call last evening, Dan is confronted with a choice. He
could make an excuse, which would help him avoid any type

of confrontation and conflict with Susan. Or he could tell her the truth, knowing full well that she is going to be annoyed.

A value will guide your decisions in various situations. Even though Dan would like to avoid conflict, he will be honest and truthful with Susan, *if* he values honesty in a relationship. His decision and his actions will reflect his underlying value for honesty in a relationship.

Values are ideas, beliefs, about what is good, what is important. Valuing is an internal process of selection or rejection based on what one believes to be good, to be important. Your values act like guides or standards which assist you in your selection of goals and the means or actions you will use to reach these goals.

If, for example, you value competition, you will most likely be attracted to school activities which are competitive in nature. You may even seek out certain friends because they also enjoy competition, whether it be in sports or school work.

Values Require Action

People can believe that they hold a certain value. The test of a true value, however, is whether or not this value is freely chosen and acted upon! Saying that you value a friendship while at the same time treating your friend unfairly, or dishonestly, would clearly be a contradiction. Valuing friendship requires that you act like a friend.

Valuing is not simply **knowing** something as right or desirable. If you have a value, then it will truly guide your decisions. You will choose and act in ways which reflect that value.

You will know something is a value when:

- You really *cherish* or feel positive about a belief or way of acting.

- You are *willing to express* your belief, or act a certain way even in public.

- You will *choose freely* to act upon a certain belief even when you have alternatives and even after considering the consequences.

- You act on your belief with *consistency* (in all situations).

If you value the relationship you have with your best friend, this relationship could be put to the "value test." Measuring your relationship against the value test should reveal that:

a. You really feel positive about the relationship (cherish it).

b. You will be happy to tell others about it (willing to express it).

c. When given the option to be with others, you would rather be with your friend (choose it freely).

d. You have acted as friends for some time (consistency).

Similarly, if a person tells you that they respect you while at the same time pressuring you to do something you truly do not want to, then there is little evidence of true respect.

This last point becomes very important in dating. Often one of the individuals is interested in necking or petting or engaging in some other type of sexual activity. The other person may not be so willing to participate. One of the individuals may say: "Oh, I'll respect you" or "If you loved me, then you would do this for me." But persons who value respect and love in a relationship will be considerate of the other person's feelings and concerns. They will not apply pressure to force others to do something that they truly do not want to do! Perhaps under these conditions it would be more accurate for someone's date to say, "I don't value you, or respect and love you, but I do value my own self-pleasure!" Somehow, hearing it this way makes it seem much less romantic, and certainly much less desirable.

Developing Values

Values are learned. From the time of your birth, your parents, your teachers, and those around you have tried to teach you certain values. You may be told hundreds of times, "Do this," or "Don't do that." These directives reflect a value held by the person teaching you. Being told to hang up your clothes or straighten your room also suggests to you that your parents value neatness, or that they respect the proper treatment of property. Often times when you live in an environment where the values are demonstrated in this way you will develop similar values.

Although many of your values start out as externally imposed rules of right and wrong, they do become internalized. As they become internalized, you will find that they guide your decisions, often without you being completely aware of their operation.

Many of your values are formed by your experience of restrictions and prohibitions. Being taught that this is wrong and that you shouldn't do this or that, helps you value what is acceptable and desirable. To some degree, even your faith provides you with ten commandments, most of which tell you what *not* to do. Yet, if you really value the prescription given by Christ, to love God, and to love your neighbor as yourself, then commandments against stealing, murdering, and so forth, really wouldn't be required. You would naturally choose not to be engaged in these types of behaviors since they are contrary to your value of loving God and loving your neighbor.

Values: Guides to Our Relationships

It is obvious that you have many different values. However, when you consider relationships, it appears that there are two values which can be considered as *primary*. These values need to guide all of your human interactions.

The ability to accept your own worth and value (self-love) and the ability to value another as having worth and value like yourself (love of others) appear to be two values essential to your development of meaningful, loving relationships. These values should not be new to you. Valuing yourself and others, regardless of race, sex, social status or *any other condition*, is what you have been directed to do by Christ. Put simply, the central value which should guide *all* of your life, as Jesus said, is to love God and to love your neighbor as yourself!

My Kind of Friend?

You may have had an experience with a person whom you thought was your friend but whom you later found out was unreliable. Perhaps you told this "friend" a secret, something very personal and private. You may have asked them never to share it with anyone else, only to find out that they spread it all around. Or perhaps this friend was the kind of person who would tell you one thing and turn around and say something completely different to another person. Or maybe you found that this special friend used you and hung around with you just to get rides to this place or that. If you have ever had such an experience, then you can appreciate that the person described is anything but a friend.

Think about the type of friend you would like to be, or the type of person you would want as a friend. Would they be people who treat you as an equal (equality)? Would they be people who were faithful (fidelity) and true (honesty) to you?

I am sure you would want friends with these values. Further, you would hope that your friends would stay true to their word (promise keeping), treat you with dignity (respect), keep up their end of bargains (responsibility), and be able to control their actions (self-control). These, like the other qualities and values listed, along with the need to be fair (social justice) and reliant (trust), are essential to healthy relationships. Because of their importance to healthy relationships, each of these values is discussed.

Equality

My family and I were watching a documentary about the late senator, Robert Kennedy. The program included a speech that Senator Kennedy gave outside a segregated restaurant. There were signs hanging up, stating, "WHITES ONLY." For many individuals, the color of a person's skin will determine his or her value as a human being.

If your behavior is guided by the value of equality, then you will act on the belief that *all people have the same rights regardless of gender, race, or creed.*

This doesn't mean that we are all equally talented or gifted in certain areas. Clearly, women are better prepared and gifted for giving birth than are men! And a tall man or a tall woman may prove to be much better at a certain job requiring height than an individual who is somewhat shorter.

Equality does not mean that every person has the right to do everything he or she wishes if he or she is not talented enough to do it. For example, Marie may not be as tall, or as strong as Jim and, as a result, may be cut from the football team. But the same may be true for Joe, who is also less physically adapted to the demands of football.

Equality would dictate that everyone who has the interest and some ability has the right to pursue that interest to the very best of his or her ability.

Equality does mean that all people have the same human value regardless of age, sex, race, or creed. God made *all* men and women as equals in His eyes! When Christ died on the cross, he did so for all individuals—*equally!*

The value of equality is essential in today's society. It is too easy for people to act as if they are superior to others. Some assume that because they have a better education or a higher income or white skin that they are better as people. It isn't so. Equality is the cornerstone of a good relationship.

Friendship is a mutual experience, not one of slave to slave master, or employee to employer. Friends are equals. They share common interests and express mutual concerns.

Fidelity

Consider a man who is a traveling salesman and away from his family. One evening he is approached by a woman who wants to have sex with him. He thinks about the fact that he is married and has children and believes that having sex with this woman would be wrong. In refusing her approach, this man demonstrates behavior which is guided by a value of faithfulness (fidelity). It is not good enough to *say* he is faithful and values fidelity and then go with this other women. The presence of his value is demonstrated *in the behavior* he chooses.

Not only must you consider if a relationship is one to which you can be faithful, you also need to consider whether that relationship allows you to be faithful *to yourself*. If you feel pressured to engage in sexual activity when inside you really don't want to, then you are not acting out of your value of fidelity. Just as you need and want your friends to be faithful to you, you must remain faithful to yourself. It is in loving yourselves the way God intends that you are able to love your neighbors.

Honesty

Telling the truth, and meaning what you say is certainly a value which God wants you to have. Honesty in a relationship doesn't mean being brutal or hurtful. If your friend asks you if you like his or her new hair cut, honesty doesn't require you to say mean or hurtful things when you don't like it.

Being honest and sensitive to the other person means being truthful about how you feel. You share that truth in a way that your friend will be able to receive it, rather than in a way that will push your friend away.

When asked if you like the new style you could say, "No, it's ridiculous, you look foolish!" Perhaps that would be truthful, and honestly how you feel. However, if you treat your friend as an *equal*, you will consider how you would feel hearing such words. This sensitivity would help you remain honest and truthful but in a more productive and sensitive way.

Guided by your values of honesty and equality, you may respond: "It isn't the type of cut that I would choose, and I think I liked the other way you had your hair, but I think it's neat that you try different things."

Promise Keeping

Building relationships and intimate friendships requires that you risk and make yourself a little vulnerable as you begin to share things about yourself that you may never have shared before. When you share such private things you need to feel that the other person can keep your confidence. Being able to keep your word and do what you say you will do (promise keeping) is a very important value in relationships.

Promise keeping is not an easy value to choose. Sometimes you are tempted to break promises because the consequence of keeping them is unpleasant. Promising your mom and dad that you won't drink at a party is good. Keeping that promise may be difficult, especially when the other kids are teasing you for being a wimp!

Or sometimes, keeping a promise is difficult when it seems so attractive to break the promise. This is the case when you know a secret and know that sharing that secret with others would give you a lot of special attention. Under these conditions, being true to your word is difficult. But being true to your word (promise keeping) is still the desirable action.

Respect

Treating another person with dignity, treating them as special, regardless of how they look, or how they act is the respect we all deserve. Being respectful, like keeping other values, is not always easy. Sometimes it is very hard to see beyond your own needs or desires in order to treat the other person with dignity, or to respect *that person's* needs and wants.

17

It is almost a cliche, but often you hear about a guy and a girl on a date where the guy is pressing the girl to "go farther" sexually. The guy then says something like, "Of course, I respect you!" My response (and I would hope it would be the girl's response) is . . ."Forget it!"

If you respect someone, then you are sensitive to their needs. You don't impose and force your wants or desires on them at their expense! If you respect someone, you don't threaten them, make fun of them, or deliberately hurt them. The boy who truly respects his date, or the girl who respects hers, will be able to say "Yes, I have a desire, *but* I don't want to force you to do something you don't want to do. I respect you!"

Responsibility

Carrying out your obligations and duties and answering for your own actions is a value which is essential to all your human development. It is easy to be responsible for your actions when those actions result in success or pleasure or a lot of praise. But if you remember, a value is something which is acted upon *consistently*. This would mean that a responsible person is also one who is accountable for his or her actions even when those actions don't lead to such a positive consequence.

Sometimes carrying out your obligations or duties cuts into your free time, or may even make you look a bit weird or different to your friends. For example, it may be "cooler" to leave your Church service early, or for that matter, not even go! But is that being responsible?

Being responsible requires courage and strength. When your strength falters, you may want to consider the struggle even Christ had with remaining faithful to his mission and his responsibility to his Father. Knowing he was about to suffer and die, Christ called out to his Father, to remove this task, to remove this responsibility. But Christ, even in the face of the pain and suffering he was about to encounter, stayed faithful to himself, and his love for us. He stayed responsible to his freely chosen duty, and thus he concluded: "Let your will be done, not mine." (Luke 22:42)

Self-Control

In order to live a value-based life, you must be able to know your alternatives. You need to understand the consequence of each alternative and *choose freely* the direction you wish to go. Choosing freely requires that you exercise self-control over your impulses.

God calls you to choose wisely. Wise choice requires time to consider and reflect on all that goes into the decision-making process. You can not do this if you are simply acting out of blind habit or impulse.

As you mature, you increase your ability to control your impulses. It may be a simple example, but consider the fact that small children often grab and touch things whenever their curiosity seems to call for it. Such a lack of impulse control can result in the child getting hurt, as might be the case of the child touching a hot pot.

There are times when you are curious, but you have learned how to choose to control your impulses in order to insure that your curiosity is both safe and appropriate. There are other desires and impulses which may feel good but which also need to be controlled. You need to value that there is a time and a place for all actions.

Adolescence is certainly the time of reflection and of the awakening of sexual feelings, but marriage is the time and place for the full expression of these sexual feelings. Delaying your desire to fulfill certain wants requires self-control. Once you see the value of self-control, you can begin to learn different strategies and activities which will help you.

Social Justice

Perhaps you have participated in some form of charity fund-raising or a clothes drive or perhaps a protest against the ill treatment of the poor. Raising money for drought-stricken farmers or the starving people in Africa or protesting the unfair treatment of political prisoners throughout the world are activities which reflect a *social justice value.*

Social justice requires you to be fair to all people. It leads you to care about all of society. It is amazing how often people can be moved to send money to a telethon or to go out to protest some unfair labor practice or even shed a tear over the malnourished infants in Africa, while at the same time being so unfair and uncaring about their next-door neighbor. Social justice requires that you care about the shy student in class or the boy or girl everyone makes fun of just as much as you are concerned for these other needy peoples. Being fair to all

19

people regardless of age, race, creed, social, economic, or political backgrounds is the essence of **loving your neighbor!**

Trust

A relationship cannot, will not, develop in an environment which is threatening and unstable. For your friendship with someone to grow, you must have trust. Trust is fostered when you can predict, with some certainty, how the other person will respond. Trust will develop in your relationships when you can act in value-directed ways.

Your Special Friend, Your Special Model

When reviewing the values and behaviors listed, you may be drawn to the reality that the truest of all friends that you and I could ever have is Jesus Christ.

Who else, besides Jesus, treated all people—sinner and repentant person, man and woman, adult and child—with such equality, respect, and social justice? Who else, that you know, even approaches the honesty, trust, faithfulness, and promise keeping that Jesus demonstrated in sharing his life, his death, and his resurrection with you? Who else, but Jesus, shows such self-control in the face of temptation and the willingness to fulfill his obligations and duties?

Christ calls out to be your friend. He provides you with a constant model and measuring stick for the kind of friend you should become and the kind of friend you should expect to have.

For Reflection and Discussion

- You can know your values by your actions! What actions do you cherish, do you willingly do and do consistently? What values might these actions suggest?

- Of all the values one might select, which two should be considered *primary?*

- Of the values discussed (equality, fidelity, honesty, promise keeping, respect, responsibility, self-control, social justice, and trust), which do you feel are essential for the development of a friendship?

- How might you demonstrate each of these values (equality, fidelity, honesty, promise keeping, respect, responsibility, self-control, social justice, and trust) daily?

Chapter 3
Male and Female: God Created Them

You must know that your body is a temple of the Holy Spirit, who is within—the Spirit you have received from God. You are not your own. You have been purchased, and at a price. So glorify God in your body.
—I Corinthians 6:19–20

Puberty, or sexual maturity, is one of the major physiological landmarks of adolescence. While it sometimes appears to happen overnight, we now know that puberty is not a sudden phenomenon. You have been sexually maturing since the moment of your conception! Cells which were to become your sexual organs, the sperm and the eggs of the next generation, were all under construction from the moment of your own conception.

Your body and your sexuality are awesome and complex creations. You have been, and are continuing to be, fashioned by the hand of God. The more you grow in understanding of that creation, the more you can appreciate how beautifully God has created you, and how you need to respect yourself, your body, and your sexuality as the temple that you are.

Puberty

While each of you will experience the body changes which accompany puberty, you may experience these changes at different times and at different rates. If there is one rule about puberty, it is that puberty provides for a lot of individual variation. This is normal. That's extremely important to remember since many teens feel anxious, or concerned, that they are developing either too fast or too slow. Remember, *your* rate is the right rate of development for you!

Most girls will start puberty anywhere between the ages of nine and fourteen. But remember, this can vary, with some of you starting younger and some later. Similarly, boys start a bit later than girls on the average, with most males entering puberty between the ages of eleven and fifteen. Regardless of starting dates and the fact that girls generally start at a younger age than boys, this is *not a race*. It is an ongoing process of development, and you all get to the place you need to be! So relax and enjoy the journey.

The Announcement

Awakening to your sexual maturity may come in a variety of ways. You may experience changes in your body appearance. For example, both boys and girls may experience the development of fatty deposits in the breast areas and the elevation of the breasts. These elevations are normal and are sometimes referred to as *breast buds*. You may even experience the presence of hair in your genital area (*pubic hair*). Or perhaps you are aware of some very sexual dreams.

All of these changes are the result of the many wonderful hormonal and physiological changes occurring during puberty. Each of these changes is an announcement of your developing sexual maturity. While these physical changes and sensations can sometimes cause you to feel awkward, or even produce some anxiety, each of these changes is a part of God's master plan and is meant to be enjoyed and truly prized!

However, with each new development and with each new gift God gives you, comes added responsibility. Learning how to respond maturely to the new physical abilities, powers, and drives you experience in puberty requires that you understand these changes and develop values which will guide you in your decisions and in the use of these wonderful gifts.

Knowledge and Understanding

"I can't believe this is happening!" "You can't get pregnant when you're fourteen." "Gosh, I only did it once. No, I can't be pregnant!"

Luckily, the young women quoted was not pregnant. However, she is dead wrong with regard to her understanding of the possibilities for becoming pregnant.

There are a lot of people, and not just teens, who simply don't understand how their bodies work. What's worse, many of these people are too embarrassed to admit their lack of knowledge. Rather than asking questions and seeking accurate information, they simply go about acting as if they know it all.

The current chapter will present you with a lot of information that you need to consider. At times, you may feel uncomfortable with the words used or the diagrams presented. That's okay. It is all right to feel uneasy about discussing this information. It is *not* okay to allow your uneasiness to keep you ignorant.

Your sexual maturity is a special gift—a gift to be developed and appreciated. It is a gift which requires special knowledge and understanding so that you may use it responsibly. Open yourself to the gift and the understanding, which highlights the many beautiful changes you are experiencing and will continue to experience.

Sexual Characteristics

The development of sexual characteristics is really the dominant feature of the teen years. Your sexual characteristics can be divided into two types: **primary** and **secondary.**

Primary Sexual Characteristics

Primary sexual characteristics are those which are related to the external and internal sex organs. For males this would include the *penis,* the *scrotum* or *scrotal sac.* (See figure 3–1a.)

25

Figure 3–1a
Male Reproductive System

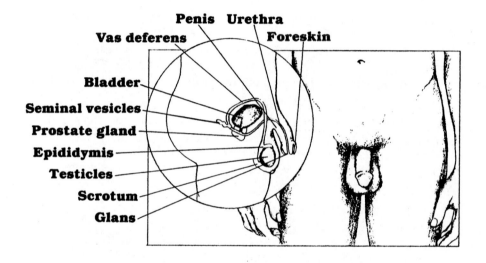

For females the primary sexual characteristics involve changes in the *mons veneris* or *mons pubis*, the *labia minor*, the *labia major*, the *clitoris*, and the *vaginal opening*. (See figure 3–1b.)

In addition to the changes in the external appearances, both males and females experience significant and wondrous changes to their internal sex organs. For males, this would involve the development and operation of the *testicles*, the *prostate gland*, and the *seminal vesicles*. For women, this would involve the structure and function of the *ovaries*, the *uterus*, the *cervix*, and the *fallopian tubes*.

Males: Primary Sexual Characteristics

The *primary sexual characteristics* in males would involve the penis and scrotum. (See figure 3–1a.)

The penis is the main sex organ for males. It is surprising that this organ which serves so many unique functions, including reproduction, elimination of body waste, and sexual pleasure, has so much misinformation spread about.

The *penis* is composed of many cavities or spaces similar to those in a sponge. Within the penis and running the length of it is a tube called the *urethra*. It is through this pathway that semen and urine pass.

When these cavities of the penis fill with blood, the penis goes from a flaccid state (unaroused) to an erect state. The rounded head or tip of the penis is called the *glans*. Some males have a piece of skin that covers the *glans*. This is known as *foreskin*. However, other males have undergone an operation (usually shortly after birth) to remove that skin. This operation is known as *circumcision*.

The average size of a mature man's penis is between three and four inches when flaccid and between five and seven inches when erect. In their flaccid state, many penises which appear smaller when compared to others may be just as large as others when erect.

Many boys become overly concerned about the size or shape of their penis. In our culture, males are sometimes made to feel that their degree of masculinity, that is the degree to which you are a male, is determined by the shape and size of the penis. That is as much nonsense as it is to suggest that you are more or less brilliant if you have a large head!

Figure 3–1b
Female Reproductive System

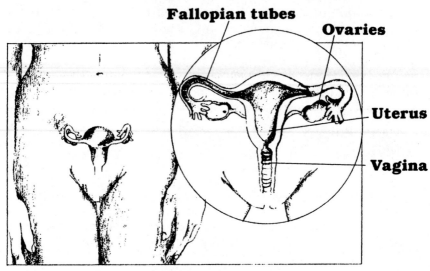

Fallopian tubes

Ovaries

Uterus

Vagina

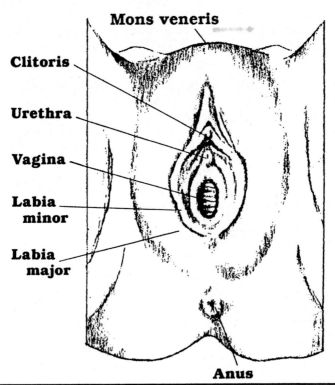

Mons veneris

Clitoris

Urethra

Vagina

Labia
minor

Labia
major

Anus

The *testicles* are often called the male sex glands, or gonads. The testicles produce sperm and male sex hormones (chemicals). The testicles are made up of hundreds of small tubes in which sperm are produced. The production of sperm does not occur until the male reaches puberty.

In the process of an *ejaculation* (the expulsion of semen and sperm from the penis), the sperm is carried from the testicles, through a tube called the *vas deferens*, to the *prostate gland*. This gland, along with the *seminal vesicle* make a milky like fluid called *semen*. During the process of ejaculation, it is the semen which travels out, carrying the sperm through the urethra.

Some people are concerned that urine and semen may go out at the same time since both use this urethra. This won't happen. There is a small valve which closes the urethra when a man urinates or ejaculates, so that the two fluids cannot go out at the same time.

Females: Primary Sexual Characteristics

For females, the *primary sexual characteristics* involve changes in the *mons veneris* or *mons pubis*, the *minor* and *major labia*, the *clitoris*, and the *vaginal opening*.

Vulva is the term applied to the genital area of women. The vulva is composed of a number of different parts. The *mons veneris* is a soft, fatty part of the genitals where the female's pubic hair grows. The opening or passage from the outside to the uterus is known as the *vagina*. The opening of the *vagina* is surrounded by folds of skin, or lips, known as the *labia*.

Below the *mons*, at the point where the inner lips meet, is the *clitoris*. This is a short organ composed of spongy tissue that can fill up with blood and become erect when stimulated. The clitoris has many nerves and is, therefore, sensitive to touch. The vaginal opening may be covered by a thin membrane called the *hymen*. Sometimes this membrane is broken as a result of the use of menstrual tampons, masturbation, sexual intercourse, or even strenuous physical activity. Some women are born without hymens.

The internal structures of the female include the primary sex glands, or *ovaries*. Like the male's testicles, ovaries serve two very important functions. The ovaries are responsible for producing female sex hormones, which are secreted directly into the blood. The ovaries are also responsible for producing the eggs (*ova*). It is truly a wonder to realize that when a girl is

ovum(1)

29

born, there are thousands of tiny egg cells in her ovaries—eggs which might someday be fertilized and develop into another human being. These egg cells are present within the girl even at birth.

The eggs are released into the *fallopian tubes* where they are carried from the ovary to the *uterus (womb)*. It is here in the *uterus* that a fertilized egg will develop into a baby. The uterus readies itself for this possibility each month by increasing the blood supply to the walls of the uterus. If pregnancy occurs, the uterus expands with the developing fetus. However, if pregnancy does not occur, the excessive blood and secretions are cleansed by way of *menstruation*.

A girl's first menstrual period, known as *menarche*, signals that her sexual maturation is nearly accomplished. It may occur as early as nine years old or as late as sixteen. Again, even with this wide range of age, there are people who start earlier, or a bit later.

At first, a girl's periods may be irregular. They may come twenty days apart or forty-five days apart. Usually, after the first year or two, a woman's menstrual cycle will become more regular, occurring every twenty to thirty-six days.

Secondary Sexual Characteristics: Males and Females

In addition to the changes in these primary reproductive organs, boys and girls experience changes in their bodies which highlight the internal maturing process and add to the distinction between males and females. Changes in appearance and body shape include the development of body parts (for example, the changing size and shape of your shoulders or hips), the development of body hair, and detectable changes in your voice. These changes are typically called secondary sexual characteristics. (See table 3–1.)

Males will notice the appearance of increased body hair on arms, legs, and chest; minor voice changes; and the first ejaculation. This first ejaculation may occur at night during sleep with a "wet dream."

A wet dream is very normal. It is one way that the body gets rid of extra sperm and semen. While women don't ejaculate, they too can have dreams which end in orgasm. But

Table 3–1
Primary and Secondary
Sexual Characteristics

Female	Male
• Underarm Hair Develops	• Underarm Hair Develops
• Pubic Hair Develops	• Pubic Hair Develops
• Wider Hips	• Wider Chest
• Rounding of Body Shape	• Increased Muscle Development
• Breasts Develop	• Development of Facial Hair
• Beginning of ovulation and Menstruation	• Voice Deepens
	• Development of Chest Hair
	• Beginning of Sperm Production and Ejaculation

since these dreams are not accompanied by ejaculation they are not called wet dreams.

Girls generally show the following sequence of secondary characteristic development. The breasts enlarge and pubic hair appears. Later, girls will develop underarm hair and continue to grow in height. With the increased height, a girl will notice that her hips become wider than her shoulders. The fatty tissue in and around the breasts, shoulders, and hips create a more rounded appearance. A girl's first menstruation will signal that her sexual maturity is near.

But How About . . . ?

. . . *INTERCOURSE?* Sexual intercourse happens when a man puts his erect penis into a woman's vagina. This action, together with the caressing that accompanies it, typically causes a peak of sexual excitement and pleasure called *orgasm.*

An *orgasm* is a feeling of pleasure that releases sexual tension. For males, the orgasm results in his penis muscles contracting and relaxing so that semen shoots from the penis in short spurts. This is called an *ejaculation*. For women, orgasm is also accompanied by muscle contractions (but not ejaculation).

The pleasure associated with sharing this very intimate experience is a reflection of the beauty and joy which God has intended for people to enjoy. But as with all the gifts God provides, we are called to be responsible recipients.

. . . *MASTURBATION?* Masturbation refers to a process by which a man or a women sexually stimulates himself or herself in order to produce sexual pleasure and orgasm.

There exists a lot of misunderstanding about the effect of masturbation on an individual. Some people, for example, have been told that if they masturbate they will go blind or go crazy or will become sterile or even develop pimples. None of this is true. There are no health risks associated with masturbation.

Because of the strong sexual feelings and desires often experienced in adolescence, as well as the fact that intercourse is typically not an option for most teens, masturbation is often used as the primary way of relieving sexual tension. While masturbation is a normal physical activity which has no evidence of causing physical or emotional harm, it is not a spiritually desirable activity.

The Catholic Church teaches that masturbation is undesirable because it tends to be a self-centered, isolating activity, which has as its only purpose self-gratification and pleasure. The Church teaches that the gift of our sexuality is provided so that we may experience an appropriate intimacy with another person in the *unitive* (making as one) experience of sexual intercourse. In addition to sharing this love and unitive experience, our sexuality is meant to serve a *creative* purpose. Both the unitive and creative elements are missing when the sexual expression takes the form of self-stimulation.

It is sometimes difficult for us to understand why something which feels so good and by all accounts is physically and psychologically normal, needs to be avoided. The point the Church makes was made clear to me by a sixteen-year-old high school junior, whom I will call Tom. In discussing the issue of masturbation with a group of teens, Tom made the following analogy. He said:

"You know, when I was much younger I used to get real angry at Adam and Eve. Don't laugh! Think about it! They had it made. I mean, they had everything they needed. They were healthy. They would never die. They lived in paradise. I mean, no school, no sickness, no hassles with careers and jobs. They had it made! And all it took to keep it going was for them not to do one simple thing God had asked."

As Tom spoke, we all began to get into the discussion. And allowing ourselves to continue with the story of Adam and Eve, we all agreed that there was probably nothing wrong with the fruit from the forbidden tree. It probably tasted good. It probably was nutritional and there probably was no physical or psychological reason why Adam and Eve should not eat it. After all, it wouldn't make them go blind or crazy or anything like that. The only reason they shouldn't eat the fruit was simply because God asked them not to!

As we discussed this, we came to realize that in a lot of ways we are like Adam and Eve. While we are not always aware of it, we are provided much in our lives. God has given us much to experience, much to enjoy. And like Adam and Eve, we have been asked to not be so selfish and self-serving, but rather to show God that we appreciate the many gifts He has bestowed.

Changes More Than Just Physical

The many physical changes which you experience in adolescence are only part of the many wonderful changes you will experience as you mature. In addition to these physical changes, there will be many psychological, emotional, and social experiences to follow. The many emotions tied to adolescence, including those of infatuation, romance, and sexual attraction can be very strong. Growing through and with them can be difficult. These feelings of attraction are discussed in the next chapter.

For Reflection
and Discussion

- What is puberty and how do you know when you have started it?

- What are the primary and secondary sexual characteristics of males? females?

- There is a lot of misinformation and misunderstanding about sexual development. Could you name one common fallacy regarding sexual development and identify how believing this could cause some real problems?

- The Church teaches that masturbation is unacceptable since it fails to serve the *unitive* and *creative* purpose of sexuality which God intended. What does this mean?

Chapter 4
Feelings of Attraction

*I plead with you, then, as a prisoner for the Lord, to
live a life worthy of the calling you have received,
with perfect humility, meekness, and patience, bearing
with one another lovingly. Make every effort to
preserve the unity which has the Spirit as its origin
and peace as its binding force. There is but one body
and one Spirit, just as there is but one hope given all
of you by your call. There is one Lord, one faith, one
baptism; one God and Father of all, who is over all,
and works through all, and is in all.*
—Ephesians 4:1–6

Most people who write about adolescence suggest that there
are two primary tasks to be achieved during these teen years.
We have already discussed one of these tasks—that is, the need
to develop a stable sense of who you are. This stable
perception of who you are is what is known as a self-concept.

In addition to revising your self-concept, you will begin to
experience the very strong desire to **share** yourself with
another person. Experiencing this drive toward *intimacy* and
learning how to responsibly and maturely respond to that
need, is the second major task of adolescence.

Your feelings of attraction and your desire to share, to be
one with another, reflect your oneness with each other, and
our oneness with God. The feelings and emotions which God
has instilled in you are intended to make life interesting and to
vitalize your relationships. Your task is to learn how to channel
these feelings, these emotions, this calling, so that your
relationships and your love reflect oneness in the Lord.

Peers

Learning to share yourself with another is an important part of your development. For most teens, their *peer group* (people of the same age) provides one major source of opportunity for such sharing. This peer group also serves a number of other very important functions.

. . . as Teachers

Your peers offer you an arena for learning and developing new skills. By watching your peers, you can learn how to dress, how to dance, how to argue, how to be cool, and even uncool. By observing your peers, you can learn how you need to act in your own social group.

. . . as Communication Practice Partners

Besides teaching you new skills, or appropriate ways of behaving, your peers also provide opportunities for you to develop your new skills. Your peers provide you the opportunity to learn and practice how to express your very strong feelings and emotions, like anger, disappointment, or even positive feelings like love. It is in your peer group that you will learn and practice those skills needed to interact with the opposite sex (including dating). And your peer group may be an excellent place for you to simply test out new ideas.

All of these skills are essential for developing a sense of who you are. Learning how to express yourself and to share intimately and act appropriately with your peers are essential for the maintenance of your generation as the next society.

. . . as Sources of Feedback

In addition to serving as coteachers and communication practice partners, your peers also provide you with feedback about how you are perceived by those outside of your family.

If you really are going to develop to your fullest, you need to begin to objectively recognize your special gifts and talents while at the same time knowing and accepting your limitations. Very often, your family members are too biased to give you the needed accurate feedback.

Moms and Dads are often blinded by the fact that you are their children. Your parents may fail to see that your clothes are really weird, or that your dancing or singing simply doesn't cut it.

Feedback can also be too negative. Perhaps your parents are too critical. Perhaps they want so much for you that everything you currently do just falls short.

In either situation, the feedback your family gives is not always as objective as you need. This is not to say that your peers are always that objective and accurate. Your peers can be biased as well. And they, like your parents, can be too positive or too critical. Often, however, your peers do provide you with some very good feedback. If you pay attention to it you may come to know yourself much better than you originally did.

That may sound funny. How can your peers know who you are better than you know yourself? Well, it's like having bad breath. Often you are blinded to your own characteristics or limitations. You may not be aware that your breath, or a certain way you act, is offensive to others, but your good friend can and hopefully will tell you. If you can respond to their feedback in a positive way then growth will occur. Growth from such feedback is not limited by just bad news or negative feedback. Feedback from your peers can be of a positive nature. Your peers may help you to see and appreciate your specialness. They may help you to become aware of the many unique gifts and talents which are yours.

It's surprising how many teens fail to recognize their own talents or gifts. Many of you may be natural leaders, or truly funny, or insightful, but you may fail to realize it. By interacting with your friends, your peers, you will come to see yourself through their eyes and begin to appreciate these gifts (along with the "bad breaths") so that you can continue to develop in the direction you wish.

The peer group is certainly a valuable resource to your healthy development. But just as the peer group provides opportunities for growth, it can also present many obstacles to your growth. Peers can also prove to be a major hindrance to your development.

True to Myself

While your friends are, and should be, extremely important to you, they should not be more important than your own emotional, physical, and spiritual health. For too many teens, being liked, being accepted by their peers, becomes too important. Perhaps you know of a person who is willing to do anything in order to become accepted.

It **is** hard to say no to drugs, or no to the sexual advances of your special friend. But, when saying yes is so destructive to you, you must say no! Wanting to belong so strongly, so desperately, invites you to be vulnerable to the negative, destructive influences of those peers who simply do not care about you but are interested only in using you.

Being popular and being accepted doesn't require you to sell out on yourself. In fact, research shows that being yourself, being happy, showing enthusiasm, indicating interest and concern for others, and showing self-confidence (*not* conceit) are the elements that contribute to popularity.

Special Friends . . . the Opposite Sex!

That's a strange phrase: the opposite sex. It almost sounds like the others are aliens. When you first start being attracted to the opposite sex, the opposite sex may seem like aliens. Teens may not know much about the opposite sex and may feel kind of strange around them.

Being attracted to another person is a very exciting and a potentially nerve-racking experience. Knowing how you feel, and how you need to respond to these feelings, is very important. The pull toward the opposite sex is an attraction which, when handled appropriately, can be enjoyable and very beneficial to your ongoing development.

Attractive?

If you were asked, which of the following characteristics would be most important to you in considering a date, which would you pick: personality, looks, intelligence, or moral character? Many surveys of teens find that personality is the characteristic most often selected. Surprised?

Interestingly though, when teens are observed in real dating situations, it appears that physical attractiveness is the most important characteristic of a date. Now perhaps we could argue that looks and personality go together and perhaps they do, but it's not important for our discussion.

Whether you are drawn to another person because of their looks, their personality, or for some other personal characteristic, doesn't matter. The feelings are intense. They can be very pleasing while at the same time very scary.

Unusual and Strong Feelings

Perhaps you have experienced being attracted to a person of the opposite sex (heterosexual attraction). You will often hear such attraction called being "turned on."

That's a great phrase. In a lot of respects, attraction to another person does turn you on. Being attracted to another turns on your bodies, your feelings, and your thoughts.

During these times, you may find your heart racing or your face flushing. It is not unusual to respond to such an attraction with sweaty palms or rapid breathing. You may feel warm inside when you are near the other person or you may experience butterflies in your stomach.

The feelings associated with attraction can be very strong and very confusing. You might find that you are more moody when you are near certain people. Or you might begin to become overly concerned about what you are wearing or how you look. You may begin to find that your mind is sometimes preoccupied by thoughts of another person. All of these feelings are normal.

It may be difficult to admit these feelings but they are normal and generally shared by everyone at one time or another. Even though these feelings may at first be somewhat uncomfortable or awkward, they will become feelings that you will begin to enjoy and perhaps even look forward to experiencing. In addition to learning to appreciate these feelings, you will also need to learn how to appropriately and maturely respond to them.

Feeling Doesn't Mean Doing

Feelings of sexual attraction can be pretty strong. This is very normal. The intensity of these feelings will vary from individual to individual and from time to time. At times, they are so strong that they are difficult to handle. But, like any of our moods, or our emotions, it is *how we handle and respond* to them that is important.

Feeling attracted to another person is not wrong. Strong sexual feelings are not wrong. They are part of being a living, healthy, human being. There are, however, appropriate and inappropriate ways of responding to these feelings.

For example, if you are angry with your best friend because he or she did not return your call, you certainly wouldn't think of punching them, or stabbing them. The anger or annoyance may be a natural reaction to not getting what you want, but responding with such violence would be inappropriate, and quite unhealthy.

The same is true for times when you are nervous or upset. Again, if you are concerned about an upcoming test you will most likely have many anxious (worrisome) thoughts and feelings. It would be doubtful, however, that you would begin to suck your thumb for security.

Desirable Responses

There are appropriate, healthy, and functional ways of responding to all of our feelings. The difficulty is that too often we don't take the time to consider all the alternative ways of responding *before* we have these feelings or before we react to the feelings.

This may be especially true when it comes to your feelings of sexual attraction. The desire to be intimate, and to be physically responsive to your sexual urges, is normal. However, becoming involved in sexual intercourse at a time when you are not physically, emotionally, socially, or spiritually prepared to deal with the consequences of such behavior is both inappropriate and unhealthy.

You need to begin to discover alternative ways to respond to your feelings of sexual attraction. Hugging, kissing, or holding hands can be beautiful experiences of shared closeness. Similarly, talking on the phone, writing special notes, or simply being with and close to another person may be wonderful ways to express and experience your attraction.

Each of these expressions of attraction may stimulate you, or the other person, to a point of wanting to go further. You need to recognize the early signs which signal that you are beginning to feel pushed in directions that you probably don't want to go.

It may sound funny but using techniques such as taking a walk, or a cold shower, or trying to think about other things like song lyrics, or prayer, are all helpful ways to reduce the intensity of your sexual urges at those times when you feel they may prove troublesome. Another strategy that you need to consider is learning how to anticipate and avoid potentially risky situations.

Dating in groups, or staying out of intimate spots (like parked cars) are strategies which can prove helpful in providing you with control over your feelings. It is a control that you need if you are going to be able to make the choices and decisions that you know are right.

Sexual attraction is a wonderful gift from God. But as with all of the gifts that our Lord provides, your sexuality and sexual attraction must be used wisely, maturely, and in ways that our Lord has intended. Such responsible use is what is meant by being stewards over the gifts God has provided.

Homosexual Attraction

For many teens, there will be a time when they feel very close, very loving, toward a person who is of the same sex. You may, for example, find yourselves enjoying a hug from that person, or enjoying sitting next to, or placing your arm around this person. You may even be curious about this person sexually.

If you have experienced this type of attraction to the same-sex person, you may be somewhat concerned. You may be concerned that you are strange or weird because of these feelings. You may even wonder whether this type of attraction means you are homosexual. The answer is no.

Homosexuality refers to individuals who are *sexually* attracted to members of the same sex. Much of what is said, or better, what is spread about homosexuality, is simply incorrect.

Stereotypes and Fears

You may have limited knowledge and understanding of homosexuality, and thus, you may tend to be fearful of it. People say that you can identify a person with a homosexual orientation simply by looking at them. It is no more true that you can identify a homosexual by his or her appearance than it is to say that you can identify a heterosexual by his or her appearance. A male who seems somewhat feminine or a female who appears to be somewhat masculine may be homosexual or heterosexual in their sexual orientation. You simply can't tell by their physical appearance or mannerisms.

Homosexuals are simply people. They are people like anyone else—with dreams and desires, insecurities and concerns. As a **group**, homosexuals are not different from heterosexuals, with one major exception. Homosexuals differ from heterosexuals only in their sexual orientation.

In addition to stereotyping homosexuals, misinformation leads many people to assume that homosexuality can be caught like a disease. While it is not absolutely certain why some people develop homosexual orientations or heterosexual orientations, it is definitely clear that neither is a contagious disease.

But Why? How?

It is not absolutely clear how or why some people have homosexual orientations. Like all of the human processes, our sexual orientation is quite complicated and complex. What sexually attracts us is influenced by a number of different factors.

Most likely, the same factors which influence the development of a heterosexual orientation create or contribute to a homosexual orientation. Currently, there are a number of different theories about the origins of our sexual orientations (either homosexual or heterosexual). One of these theories would suggest that our sexual orientation is biologically determined—that it involves our genes and our hormones and even our brain chemistry.

A second theory suggests that our environment, specifically our family, plays a very important role in the development of our sexual orientation. A third view of what causes homosexuality is much more complex. This position suggests that sexual orientation is a result of an ongoing developmental process. That is, as you and I develop from birth, a number of events—both internal and external, biological, social, and psychological—come to play in the creation of our very unique self. The fact that you are born with certain genes, into a particular household, within a specific community, at this time in our world and human history, all means that you will experience events which will come to play in your creation. All of these factors are different from those which I or others will experience, and thus, your uniqueness.

This developmental perspective would argue that as you and I develop we begin to discover and make decisions about our bodies, our sexual identity, how we view ourselves as male or female, and how we feel we should relate to the same and the opposite sex. It is this very complex set of perceptions, experiences, and decisions that results in our eventual sexual identity and sexual orientation.

Not so simple, is it? There is no one clear, single cause and effect that can explain homosexuality. While it is not important for us to understand the details of these theories, it becomes quite clear that for most people today homosexual orientation is not a disease or a curse or even sinful. It is a state of a very complicated, complex process of human development.

The Church and Homosexuality

But what does the Church say about homosexuality? Doesn't the Bible condemn homosexuals?

If you have watched the news or read the papers recently, you begin to see that many Churches, and "religious" people have condemned homosexuals and made them feel unwelcome within their Church.

Often people point to the Bible as evidence that homosexuality is sinful. While we are not even going to attempt to understand or discuss the subtle intentions and meanings of the Bible, what is clear is that there are places in the Bible where heterosexual activities (in addition to homosexual activities) are similarly viewed as sinful.

The Catholic Church teaches that genital sexual activity and intercourse, are intended as expressions of love, to be shared by two individuals within the committed union of the marriage vows. Thus, intercourse outside of marriage, and masturbation, fail to fulfill this *unitive* purpose of sex. Such out-of-marriage sexual experiences are considered wrong.

The Church also teaches that God created sex for procreation as well as for the expression of love between husband and wife. Homosexual activity cannot fulfill the *procreative* purpose of sex.

Both homosexuality and heterosexual intercourse outside of marriage are considered morally wrong. Homosexuality fails to satisfy the procreative function of sexuality, and heterosexual intercourse outside of marriage fails to fulfill the unitive purpose of sex.

While the Church is clear that such activity, such behavior, is morally wrong, the point that needs to be made is that people with homosexual orientations are not sinners or horrible people simply because of that orientation. The Bible clearly commands that the male homosexual act not take place. However, it does not command a man not to be a homosexual or even to have homosexual feelings. It is the act which is condemned, not the orientation.

If you feel the need to condemn and perhaps punish people with homosexual orientations because you think they are sinners, then you need to really consider what is meant by the greatest of all commandments: to love God and to love your neighbor as yourself. Regardless of our sexual orientation, we are people, made in the image and likeness of God. Each of us, regardless of our sexual orientation, reflects the love of God. As such, each of us deserves to be treated with dignity and respect.

Your task as Christians is to attempt to understand people with homosexual orientations and respond to them with the *same* love and care you would have for any other person who is your neighbor. Homosexuals, like heterosexuals, are called by God to respond to His invitation to come follow Him. How they seek and follow God's will, given their realities and their choices, is *between them and God.*

For Reflection and Discussion

- Peers can serve a number of very important functions. They are teachers, communication practice partners, and sources of feedback. In what ways has your own peer group served these functions for you?

- Sexual attraction is sometimes referred to as being "turned on." In what ways does being attracted to someone make you alive and turned on?

- There are many stereotypes about homosexuality. Choose one such stereotype and discuss how it is inaccurate.

- The desire to be close and intimate is normal. What are some of the ways you could be close and intimate without sexual contact?

Chapter 5
Equality of Males and Females

*All baptized in Christ, you have all clothed
yourselves in Christ, and there are no more
distinctions between Jew and Greek, slave and free,
male and female, but all of you are one in Christ
Jesus.*
—Galatians 3:27–28

When people talk about sexuality, most often they think of the physical characteristics of a person. A person's sexuality involves much more than simply the presence of genitals and physiological structures. Sexuality involves much more than biology and anatomy.

In addition to how you look and how you are built physically, your sexuality is defined by the way you act, and the way you are expected to act because of your gender. Those ways of acting, and the way people expect you to act because of your gender, either male or female, constitute what is known as your *sex role*.

Factors Influencing Sex Role Development

It used to be assumed that one's sex role behaviors were simply determined by his or her biology. The fact that boys' and girls' genetic makeup was different and that they had different types of hormones was used as an explanation for why males or females acted differently from each other.

47

Biological Factors

Biological factors, such as one's chromosomes (X or Y), and the presence of certain sex hormones, clearly contribute to the differences noted between male and female development and behavior. However, biology is not the only nor perhaps the most important influence on sex role development.

Environmental Factors

Most researchers would argue that biology combines with environmental factors to create your sex role. These environmental factors include the effects of your *socialization*, *parental modeling*, and *cultural messages*.

Socialization

The process by which you learn the rules and expectations of society, along with the right and proper ways of behaving in society, is known as socialization. Often this socialization, or social education, is very obvious. This is the case when you are told very directly the rules of driving. Often, however, the rules of society are taught in much more subtle, less obvious ways.

In our culture, adults begin to discriminate between boys and girls almost from birth. Adults treat newborn boys quite differently from the way they treat baby girls—the old "pink and blue" treatment.

These may seem like little things, but each of these different ways of being treated provides unique experiences which in turn communicate to us how we are to act. The different ways we choose a newborn's clothes, hairstyle, toys, and so on, all act as subtle influences on how we will treat that infant. The way we treat the infant will cause him or her to respond in certain ways. So, for example, if we give a little girl a baby doll to play with we are encouraging her to develop play skills which are quiet, gentle, and mothering in appearance. Whereas, if we give a little boy a football, we are encouraging him to develop behaviors which are more physical, competitive, and generally rough and aggressive.

The way we treat the sexes differently can be seen in things such as: little girls get dollies, little boys have trucks. Little infant girls have nice dresses and bows in their hair; boys have overalls and their hair combed flat. This differential treatment isn't required for the healthy development of the two individuals. However, such treatment does teach us to see the sexes as separate and different.

Surely, boys and girls are different. The socialization process which teaches us this difference is not a matter of concern. However, when the lesson of difference is also a lesson of *inequality*, then we must be concerned. Saying that one thing is different from another thing doesn't mean that one thing is better. It simply means that these two things are different. Often people assign values to different things. So that what was once simply "this" or "that," as two different things, becomes valued as "good" and "bad," or "good" and "better."

Because you are trained to see differences, and since differences can sometimes be falsely labeled as unequal, it is important for you to begin to understand how you are taught to distinguish and perhaps discriminate between the sexes and to remember that we are all one in Christ Jesus.

Parental Modeling

Your parents serve as one of the major sources of your socialization. They may serve as the primary teachers of your sex role. Your parents teach you directly how they would like you to respond. Perhaps they told you that "little boys don't cry" or that "little girls are not supposed to play rough." In addition to directly teaching you sex role behaviors, your parents also teach you what is expected by the way they act.

Modeling is the process by which we learn how to act by observing another. Little boys are encouraged to model, or imitate, their dads. Little girls get rewards for acting like little mommies! Learning to imitate your same-sex parent helps to perpetuate and pass on certain sex role behaviors.

Cultural Messages

In addition to your parents, there are other channels through which expected sex role behavior is conveyed to you. Throughout your life, you will be bombarded by subtle and sometimes very obvious sex role messages.

For example, some of the books you used in school for reading class had stories in which little girls were presented as playing with dolls and playing house while describing boys as playing ball or wrestling. The same books may even suggest that little girls are better at writing and English, whereas boys are supposed to be stars in mathematics and science.

Our culture also conveys expected sex role behavior through the media. This includes the print media, television, advertisement, and even music.

Sex Role Stereotypes

It may sound somewhat silly to say, but girls are different from boys. The question is, are they as different as might be assumed? Often a person is labeled and assumed to have certain characteristics simply because he or she is a member of a certain group. This is known as *stereotyping.*

Stereotyping—The Goods and Bads

Stereotyping may help us simplify our very complex world. If we can simply assign a label to a person, then we don't have to consider or think about their complexity and uniqueness. The problem with stereotyping is that often our labels are simply incorrect.

It might be a meaningful exercise to watch television commercials for a week, or pay special attention to the stories in your English class, in order to develop a picture of males and females as presented by these media. You may become aware that the images, the pictures, the sex roles, that are presented to you are not always accurate. You may find that the male or female they describe is **not** you. You may even find that you possess some of those behaviors and traits supposedly assigned to the opposite sex. If this is true, don't worry. You're not wrong, or strange—the sex role stereotype **is!**

Worse than simply being incorrect, stereotypes are often near impossible to correct or break once they have been applied to a person. You may treat a person a certain way without provocation just because of the stereotype. Or the person may even begin to believe that they are just like the label implies. Stereotyping destroys the beauty and wonder of the uniqueness of each human. Stereotyping can damage an individual.

Consider the teen who is labeled "queer" or "gay" or a "sissy." The label, once heard, may cause the boy to be rejected by those who don't even know him, even when the label is inaccurate.

Stereotypes not only cause tremendous emotional upset but can really undermine the person's own opinion about himself or herself.

Fact or Myth?

It certainly can be demonstrated that boys and girls do differ in a number of significant ways. For example, females are generally found to be biologically stronger than males and may have a greater life expectancy. As a group, boys are more aggressive than girls, perform better on standardized math tests than girls, and demonstrate less verbal ability than girls on those same tests. **Be careful,** however!

Notice that this is as a *group. Individual* boys and girls, you and I, may not fit this pattern at all. Further, even if the group does appear stronger or weaker on some characteristic behavior, that does not mean that it is a *natural, inborn, gender-based* difference. Most of the characteristics that are used to distinguish boys and girls are a function of learning, experience, and socialization. They are not innate or inborn differences.

Girls and boys can be *equally* strong, sensitive, bright, achieving, independent, and creative if given the opportunity to exercise these traits.

Sexism

Often the presumed differences between two groups of people become evaluated as better or worse. When one sex is considered superior, and discrimination and prejudice against the other sex results, we have a form of social injustice known as *sexism.*

You may have experienced sexism in your own life. Have you ever been prevented from doing something you wanted to do simply because you were a boy or a girl? Not being able to play with certain toys or cry publicly or not being able to join this team or apply for this job just because you are a girl or boy is *sexism.*

If you have experienced such prejudice and discrimination, then you know how painful and how destructive it can be. In addition to the pain you experienced, sexism also restricted the benefits that you could have brought to that team, that job, your world!

It is wrong to restrict an individual from developing his or her potential and pursuing his or her talents and interests. Sexism and sex role stereotyping does exactly this. Historically, women have been treated as inadequate or as inferior to men. Similarly, American men have been restricted free expression of their feelings and emotions, being taught to believe that such expression is a sign of weakness.

Being able to pursue any career one desires regardless of one's gender has enabled individuals to develop their talents to a maximum. The freedom to become a nurse, a secretary, a child-care worker, or a teacher has opened up these valuable professions to many men who previously felt intimidated or restricted from involving themselves in these careers. Similarly, enabling qualified women to become physicians, executives, mechanics, and so on, has added to the quality of our work force. Restricting a person's rights and freedom, as in the case of not being free to pursue a chosen career because of one's gender, is not only destructive to the individual but to our entire society.

Sexism is harmful! It limits human potential and is certainly contrary to God's plan.

Sexual Equality

Recently our society, our culture, and our world have begun a number of significant changes in the way we view males and females. We have begun to become more sensitive to the way sex role stereotypes impact each of us.

For example, employment opportunities are no longer classified by sex, so that doors that have been previously closed to one sex or the other are now beginning to open. Even though the removal of such sex-discriminating barriers is a step in the right direction much more needs to be done in order to achieve true human equality.

While it is clear that males and females are different, it is similarly true that males and females are more alike than different. In fact, many researchers today argue that we should change the way we view masculine and feminine traits.

52

It is suggested that we should stop viewing masculine and feminine traits as two separate factors, which you either have or you don't have. Rather, it is argued that we should see our sex role identities as falling on a continuum. This continuum would have at one extreme people who demonstrate more masculine and less feminine traits. Toward the middle of the continuum would be a position where the traits are equally distributed. At the other end of the continuum would be people who exhibit mostly feminine and few masculine traits. This approach to viewing masculinity and femininity, as traits exhibited by all individuals regardless of their gender, is known as an *androgynous view*.

Equal in the Eyes of God

People who believe in such an *androgynous view* feel that every male has and should have some characteristics or traits which have previously been described as feminine. Similarly, every female has and should have some masculine attributes. An androgynous individual is one who has the best of both worlds. They are achievement oriented, show high self-esteem, and are warm, sensitive, and nurturing.

The point which needs to be highlighted is that it isn't important that you be this way, that way, or both ways. Rather, you need to be fully human, in touch with all of your potential and become all that you can be.

There is no better or worse fixed sex role behavior. There is no better or worse gender. There are only people. People who, regardless of their differences, are **equal in the eyes of God!**

For Reflection and Discussion

- Sex role, or the way you are expected to act because of your gender, is determined by a number of factors or influences. What are they?

- What are some of the ways your family teaches boys to be boys and girls to be girls?

- What is a sex role stereotype? Give some examples of sex role stereotyping and show how these stereotypes are not only inaccurate but potentially damaging.

- What is sexism? Can you give a personal example of where you may have experienced sexism?

Chapter 6
Making Decisions

"For me there are no forbidden things"; maybe, but not everything does good. I agree there are no forbidden things for me, but I am not going to let anything dominate me. Food is only meant for the stomach, and the stomach for food; yes, and God is going to do away with both of them. But the body—this is not meant for fornication; it is for the Lord, and the Lord for the body. God, who raised the Lord from the dead, will by his power raise us up too.
—I Corinthians 6:12–14

Decisions, decisions, decisions! If nothing else, adolescence is certainly a time when you are faced with a number of choices and decisions. Choosing properly so that you don't let "anything dominate " you is sometimes very difficult.

The choices you make during the next few years can have serious consequences. For example, choosing to just try a drug once can be life-threatening. Choosing to have sex can lead to very permanent and life-impacting consequences, including things such as getting pregnant or contracting a venereal disease.

All of your decisions will result in some form of consequences. It is important for you to consider all the implications of your choices *prior* to making them.

God has given you the power to choose. Make decisions which choose God. God has given you the gift of love. Make decisions which allow you to love—yourself, your neighbor, and your God—as Jesus would have you love.

The Decision-Making Process

Making decisions is a difficult process. For years, it was believed that some people were simply born with the ability to make good, rational decisions. We now know that rational decision making is a process which is learned. And even though most schools don't offer a course in decision making, it is something which you can teach yourself once you understand some very basic principles. Like many things you learn, developing a decision-making model will at first seem somewhat artificial. It won't feel natural because you haven't made it yours. However, the more you use it, the more it will become natural. Eventually, it will become a part of you and will kick into operation without much thought or energy on your part.

The method of decision making described below involves six separate steps.

1. Problem Identification

2. Impulse Delay

3. Path Finding

4. Evaluation

5. Selection

6. Re-evaluation

Step 1: Problem Identification

The first step to decision making is to *identify the problem* that you are attempting to resolve. A clear goal is necessary for responsible, rational decision making.

Many people, and not just teens, fail to clarify their goals *prior* to making a decision. It is as if they impulsively respond without first thinking about what it is they *really* are trying to achieve. Now this may seem like an obvious and easy step. After all, we all know what we want. Or do we?

Consider the situation where you and your parents have been disagreeing about a time for curfew. For the sake of our discussion, let's pretend that they want you to be in by nine P.M. and you want to stay out until ten P.M.

At first glance, we may assume that there is a simple resolution to this problem. It may seem that all that needs to be done is for you and your parents to compromise. Curfew could be set at nine-thirty P.M. and that would be that!

The decision to set curfew at nine-thirty works *only if* the problem is one of simple mathematics. This solution works only if the problem is one of finding a point equidistant from both time limits.

But what happens if your goal isn't really to stay out until ten? What happens if staying out until ten o'clock is really a strategy or a way for you to achieve another goal? Maybe your real goal is to insure that you don't feel different than your friends. Perhaps your friends stay out until ten and you feel like a wimp having to leave early.

In this case, coming home at nine-thirty doesn't work. Similarly, staying out until ten may not be the only strategy for achieving your goal. For example, what if your friends had to be home by nine or what if your friends started to come to your house. Then you wouldn't feel like the one who stands out as different.

Just to be fair, let's consider the same example from the parents' vantage point. Let's pretend that the goal for your parents is not really to have you in by nine, but rather to feel that you are safe. In this case, the goal is to feel secure. Your parents hope to achieve a sense of security that you are all right. The nine o'clock curfew is only one strategy for achieving this goal.

Once we have identified your parents true goal, we will be able to discover other strategies which will allow them to gain their goal of knowing you're safe, but in a way that would be more acceptable to you. Could you think of some?

One alternative might be for you to let them know where you are. Another would be for you to demonstrate that there is adult supervision or that there is a safe way for you to get home. With these conditions set in place, your parents might feel that their goal of knowing you are safe is secured regardless of whether the curfew is nine o'clock or ten o'clock.

Learning to separate our goals from our strategies is often quite difficult, and takes practice. This can be especially true when it comes to decisions about sexual behavior. Often teens want to feel loved or accepted; as a result, they may misinterpret these feelings as the need (goal) to have sex.

Wanting to be loved or accepted is a valid need for intimacy. However, our natural drive toward intimacy can be achieved through strategies other then sexual contact. Deeply sharing with another, opening up and being vulnerable with a friend, holding another and being close with another, can all be methods for achieving and experiencing intimacy.

But before you could decide that one of these alternatives would prove successful, you would need to be aware that it is intimacy or closeness or a feeling of belonging that you desire and not sexual contact.

Step 2: Impulse Delay

In order to make the best decisions possible, you need *time* to consider all the possible alternatives and the consequences for each alternative. Then you can make a rational conscious decision regarding the path you wish to follow.

This requires time and energy in order to consider all the needed information. This process requires that you delay your tendency to respond impulsively and nonreflectively!

Like the other parts of this rational decision-making process, *impulse delay* is not as easy as it may first appear. For most of us, when we want something, we want it now.

As a small child, you were probably very impulsive. You would grab or take or stick or push for whatever you wanted. Oftentimes, your impulsive actions caused you pain. Perhaps you touched a hot stove or broke a toy or made yourself sick because you reacted without much thought or consideration.

Happily, as you grew older, you also developed the ability to control your impulses. But controlling these impulses takes energy and sometimes, not responding immediately may make you feel a bit uncomfortable. But controlling your impulses is *essential* for your healthy development.

Just think about the two-year-old child. When that child feels pressure on the bladder, she or he reflexively and somewhat impulsively wets. As little children learn to impose control on their reflex or impulse tendency, they learn not to wet their pants. Initially, this is not very much fun; after all, when you have to go, you have to go!

However, learning to control his or her impulses also enables this child to have the opportunity to experience staying dry, not having to wear diapers, not having the inconvenience of constantly changing clothes, avoiding diaper rash, and even earning new freedoms, such as being able to go to school, or spend the night at a friend's house. Controlling your impulses leads to much more healthy decisions and, ultimately, to much richer experiences.

The same can be true with your sexual impulses. When you experience a sexual urge, it will often be experienced as extremely strong and impelling. The immediate impulse may be to respond to that strong desire or urge by masturbating or by becoming sexually active with another. While giving in to your impulse may relieve the pressure of the sexual urge, it may also lead to consequences which are less than desirable. Impulsively having sex whenever, and with whomever, you desire exposes you to sexually transmitted diseases, makes you vulnerable to becoming pregnant, and most importantly, takes you away from God's invitation to follow Him.

Learning to control your impulses provides you the time and the energy needed to consider the various options available for meeting your needs, as well as the consequences for each of the possible strategies.

In order to control your impulses, you need to begin to interrupt the cycle, or the connection between *need and immediate response*. When you experience an urge or a need, you literally need to stop, count to ten, and ask yourself, "What is it I am feeling?" "What is it I wish to achieve?" and "What are the various ways I can reach my goal?"

Counting to ten may seem like a silly, childish solution. Yet, the process of counting to ten can be a powerful and useful tool for interrupting your need-response cycle. The technical name for such a technique is *refocusing*.

Refocusing is a technique in which you use one way of thinking, such as counting or singing or praying, to interrupt another way of thinking. For example, if you are thinking about something that may be sexually stimulating and wish to stop, focusing on another thought will interfere and stop the sexual fantasy. You can also use refocusing to help you respond with a cooler head at times when you are angry.

Whenever your emotions are running very high and very intensely, you need to stop and refocus your thinking in order to reduce the intensity of your feelings. Intense emotion will block your rational decision making and encourage your impulsive responding.

Step 3: Path Finding

Once you have clearly identified what your needs are and what it is you hope to achieve, you need to begin to identify the various strategies, or *paths*, that you can take to achieve that goal.

Path finding is a process in which you identify a number of possible alternative paths or routes to goal attainment and problem solution. There are a number of techniques which you can use to assist you in generating such paths. One technique is called *brainstorming*.

While brainstorming is best used with more than one person, you can use a modified version by yourself. The procedure is simple. The goal is to generate as many solutions as possible. It is important to allow yourself to think as creatively as possible. The ideas do not even have to make sense or be possible to implement. That's what is meant by "storming." Just let as many ideas as possible flood your brain. What you will find is that if you allow yourself to think creatively without evaluating your ideas, you will begin to develop some very good alternatives.

So, for example, if you were trying to identify *paths* for reducing your sexual urge you might start to list some of the solutions found in table 6–1. Remember, the solutions do not have to be possible, nor even desirable. You will evaluate each of the possible paths in the next step of the decision-making process.

Step 4: Evaluation

During the evaluation step, you need to review each of the possible paths in terms of their consequences. You need to ask yourself "what if" I do this or that strategy? You need to consider the consequences of each strategy as if you had a special means of seeing the future.

Table 6–1

Example of Path Finding

Need: Reduced sexual urge

Paths:

- masturbate

- engage in sexual contact with another

- go to sleep and hope for nocturnal emission or sexual orgasm

- think it away

- exercise to reduce the tension

- take a cold shower

- jog

- use thought stopping

- bear with the urge as a form of self-sacrifice and prayer

- pray for strength to avoid giving in to the impulse

- become socially active, play a game, talk on the phone, go visit someone, until the urge passes

---

The consequences you need to consider for each of the alternatives include such things as benefits gained by you or by others who may be involved, problems which may result from this strategy for you or others, feelings that may result from one strategy or another, or the costs (emotionally, financially, physically, spiritually) which are involved with each of the strategies.

Your evaluation of each of the strategies can be facilitated by asking yourselves the following questions.

- How will I feel if I use this solution?

- What will happen after I use this strategy?

- What will it cost me or how will it affect me, both in the short and long term?

- Which of the solutions is most effective in not only solving my immediate problem but in leading me in the direction I want to take as a young Christian man or woman?

Table 6–2 provides one example of how this evaluation can look.

Table 6–2
Example of Path Evaluation Process

Path/Strategy	How will I feel	Costs	Impact on bringing me closer to God
Intercourse	sexually satisfied dissatisfied with lack of self-control	possible sexually transmitted diseases possibility of pregnancy bad reputation	moves me away from God missed an opportunity to demonstrate desire to be Christ-like
Refocusing (e.g., pray or concentrate on reading a book)	sexually frustrated (short period) feel in control feel proud	none, except minor discomfort	feel closer to God appreciate the temptation Christ endured for us

Steps 5 and 6: Selection and Re-evaluation

Even though you may try your best to anticipate the consequence of each of the paths you have generated, you may not be as completely accurate as you would have liked. Quite often, as a result of your decisions, things happen which you could not have anticipated.

After you have selected the path which appears to be the best and have implemented that strategy, you need to assess the various impacts.

You may wonder why you need to re-evaluate your selection after it is over. There are two benefits to re-evaluation. First, even though this event or this specific situation may never occur again, the *type* of situation, or the general kind of decision, will be experienced again. You may be able to learn something from your past experience that makes the next time all that much better.

Secondly, by getting into the habit of re-evaluating, you train yourself to be better able to predict consequences during the original evaluation stage of the decision-making process.

One strategy that I have found useful in this *re-evaluation* is the process known as *instant replay*. In instant replay, you review the event and your decision as if you were watching it on television. You may have heard people say that they are great Monday-morning quarterbacks. Or they may say: "If I only knew then what I know now, I would have acted or decided differently!"

Using the *instant replay* method, you rethink, in as much detail as possible, a situation and a decision with which you struggled. You try to remember as much as possible about the setting, the time, the things leading up to the decision, and the things surrounding the decision, along with your feelings at the time.

In addition to describing the external events leading up to the situation, you also attempt to re-establish how you felt and what you were thinking about at the time. You try to answer the question, "What did I think to myself about the situation?" "What did it mean to me?"

Then you replay the entire situation in your mind. You try to see options or alternatives that were available to you. It is important to really look for these options, these alternatives. Practicing looking for alternatives in your instant replay, while not changing the reality of your initial decision, does help you practice being an *alternatives* thinker.

A good example of this type of thinking can be found in case 6–1.

Case 6–1
Instant Replay

Coleen was a seventeen-year-old high school senior with whom I was working. Coleen was a good student, popular with her classmates, and generally involved in many school activities. For all her talents and good traits, Coleen didn't always feel good about herself and often needed somebody to tell her (or show her) that she was worthwhile.

Coleen had recently made a very big decision in her life. After struggling for some time to remain a virgin, Coleen found herself in a situation in which the struggle was hard to maintain. She had decided to have sex with a boy whom she had been dating for four months.

When we discussed the situation and the decision in the form of an instant replay, a number of insights were gained by Coleen. In the instant replay, Coleen was quite detailed and descriptive. She said: "I know that the night we went out, we had a small fight. Tommie told me that he felt I was the only girl he ever really loved. He also told me that he had never dated a girl for as long as four months. It was our anniversary and Tommie was pressuring me to go to a motel with him.

"I explained to him that I really thought I loved him, but that I wasn't ready. We drove around and eventually got some beer.

"We went to the park and were listening to some music and we started to make out. Tommie kept trying different things and I kept telling him no. Then I remember at one point, he stopped kissing me and started crying just a little.

"We talked and he told me how much he really needed me . . . and that if I loved him, I would know it was all right.

"I could hear myself thinking 'Oh, I'm going to lose him. What's wrong with me? Everybody does it! Why am I so weird? After all, I do love him!' And then the next thing I knew, I stopped saying no."

As we reviewed the instant replay, Coleen was quick to note a couple of places where there were options that she hadn't realized at the time.

For example, she noted:

1. *"When Tommie said, 'If you loved me you would know it was right.' I could have responded, 'If you loved me you would appreciate how wrong it feels for me.'"*

2. *"I know it sounds like a cop out, but drinking the beer kind of lowered my defenses. I could have refused to drink it."*

3. *"I needed to argue with myself. I had myself convinced that I desperately needed Tommie. I mean, I do really like him, but if I lost him it would not be the end of the world."*

Coleen could identify quite a few more spots in which she could have made other decisions. Each of these alternative decisions would have led to a different consequence. In addition to identifying the alternative decisions she could have made, Coleen also evaluated the possible consequence of each of these alternatives. This evaluation of consequences not only helps you choose the best option but also teaches you to think ahead.

Perhaps you could think of a few more alternatives Coleen had available.

Christian Conscience— Values and Decisions

In addition to considering the positive and negative consequences of your decisions, you will find that your decisions are also guided by your *values*. Selecting a path is and should be influenced by your sense of right and wrong.

Like Coleen, knowing what is right, what is desirable, what is God's basic direction, is often not enough to guide all your decisions. You need to continue to develop and strengthen your Christian conscience, so that it becomes a major influence in your decision making.

If you are to be guided by the principles established and modeled by Jesus, you must first *know* these principles. Knowing Christ, like truly knowing any good friend, requires that you develop a personal relationship with Christ. It is not as simple as memorizing the Ten Commandments. You need to translate the messages found in Scripture into your own personal language. You need to take the Jesus of the Bible and make him a personal friend.

Following the basic values and Christian teachings will help you make choices in relationships, choices which are in agreement with the choices Jesus would have made in a relationship. Choosing in ways which reflect your respect for the dignity of yourself and others is the way God has directed you.

Thinking about the consequences of your choices and decisions will help you select a particular path. Thinking about the directive given you by God—to love God, and to love your neighbor as yourself—will help you make decisions in relationships. These decisions will then bring you closer into loving relationship with yourself, with others, and with your God!

For Reflection and Discussion

- What are the six steps to be used in problem solving?

- Controlling your impulses is a difficult yet necessary process. Why is it so important to control your impulses? Can you give an example of a technique you could use to control your impulses?

- What is the process known as brainstorming? What are the rules to follow when brainstorming?

- Discuss one decision you recently made. Using the Instant Replay Technique, do you see other options or choices you could have made?

Chapter 7
Developing
Relationships

Be at peace among yourselves. And this is what we
ask you to do, brothers [and sisters]: warn the idlers,
give courage to those who are apprehensive, care for
the weak and be patient with everyone. Make sure
that people do not try to take revenge; you must all
think of what is best for each other and for the
community. Be happy at all times; pray constantly;
and for all things give thanks to God, because this is
what God expects you to do in Christ Jesus. Never
try to suppress the Spirit or treat the gift of prophecy
with contempt.
—I Thessalonians 5:13–20

Making friends and developing relationships is not only
psychologically healthy, it is spiritually fulfilling. As Christians,
we are called to love one another. We are called to become
one, to become community, brothers and sisters in Christ.
However, finding and making new friends, forming
relationships, or finding a special someone are not easy tasks.

If you are like most teens, you probably have experienced
times when you wished that the process were easier. It can be
a lot of work meeting, making, and *keeping* a friend.

Initially, most of our friends are really only brief, superficial
contacts but eventually some of these contacts do become very
close, special friends. Dating, dances, and the various social
and school activities all provide the arena for the identification
and development of friendships.

Dating: A Special Way of Relating

Dating is a relatively recent phenomenon. Some researchers have suggested that dating, as you know it, really didn't exist prior to the 1920s. Prior to 1920, "dates" were carefully monitored by parents. Parents would control the nature of the contact. During this period, dates may have involved a nice dinner at your house, or going with the family to the Church social. Sound like fun? Well, it was fun, just a different type of fun! Historically, dating served only one major purpose and that was to select a mate. Today, dating serves a number of purposes, in addition to mate selection and courtship.

Dating as Recreation

Dating can be simply a form of recreation. For most teens, dating is fun (at least after the initial uneasiness passes!). It is a real source of enjoyment and generally a fun way to fill time.

Dating for Social Status

Dating can also be viewed as a way of achieving status among one's friends. Taking the best-looking guy or gal or the star athlete or the head of the student government to the prom may be a way to get some special recognition or even increase status among one's friends. Sometimes, being the first to date is also a way of getting some status.

Dating as Social Training

Dating is also a very normal and needed part of learning how to get along with one another. Dating provides teens with the opportunity to practice those skills needed to become more mannerly and sociable.

This social-training function of dating is quite evident during times of those special dates, such as at proms or at Christmas and homecoming dances. These important events help teens learn how to act appropriately in a social setting.

Dating as Courtship

Finally, dating remains the primary process by which one selects a future mate. This is called the courtship function of dating. Through dating, a person begins to narrow down from those many people to whom he or she is attracted to that one special individual with whom that person may some day decide to share his or her life.

The Developing Relationship

While we sometimes believe that friends just happen or that Prince and Princess Charming fell magically and permanently in love at first sight, the truth is that relationships all grow and dissolve in predictable and understandable phases. Generally, relationships develop in small steps or stages, moving from superficial contact ("Hi, what's your name?") through some personal sharing ("My favorite group is . . . how about yours?") to more depth, more sharing, more intimacy. Not every relationship will proceed through all the stages, but it is useful to understand the process of relationship development so that you can better understand your reactions and frustrations with your own relationships.

Initiation

The first step in developing any relationship is making contact (initiation). For some, this is one of the most painful and awkward steps in relationship building. Coming up with a way to initiate contact is not always easy.

Since first impressions can be so influential in the development of a relationship, you need to open or initiate with whatever comes naturally and genuinely. A simple "Hi, my name is. . . ." or even "I'm a little nervous, but I wanted to introduce myself," will prove a lot more productive in the long run then some manufactured line.

Experimenting

After meeting a person, you need to decide whether or not you want to risk sharing yourself and developing a relationship with this person. During this stage, you will do a lot of small talking. You may begin to ask your newfound friend questions such as: "Where are you from?" or "What music do you like?" or "Hey, do you know (name one of your other friends)?"

71

This period of experimenting is a safe way to test the water. It is a way to get to know if you and this other person have anything in common. It is during these early stages of your relationship that you test whether you want to go further in your experiment of friendship building.

Too often this *friendship-building function* of dating is lost to sexual pressure. Rather than learning about each other and sharing emotionally, socially, intellectually, and spiritually, teens become blinded by the pressure to share physically. It is hard to resist that pressure but the value of resisting is that it allows for a fuller development of the relationship.

Dating needs to be approached as a key process in the development of friendships. If teens consider dating as a relationship-building process, a process for developing special friends, as opposed to lovers, they will find that their dating is much more productive.

Intensifying

Through continuing contact with a friend, you will come to know much more about the other person, much more about their private interests and wants. The relationship is no longer one of simple, friendly acquaintance, but one which is marked by personal intensity.

Integrating

As a dating couple continues to experiment with friendship building, they will end up spending more and more time together, finding more and more in common. They may start to highlight their similarity by dressing alike or talking in similar ways, using their own special phrases or words. Others may start to treat them as if they were a pair.

When a boy and girl move into the integrating stage of a relationship, they start to be identified as dating, and friends usually refer to them as a unit. Rather than seeing Kathy and Joe as two individuals it becomes "Kathy-n-Joe."

During this stage of their relationship, couples begin to develop points of common reference such as "our song" or "our place."

Bonding

If the relationship continues to grow in depth, a couple generally wants to make a more formal commitment to one another and have this commitment recognized by others. Teens who are bonding will attempt to have signs or symbols which announce to those around them that they are committed to each other. For example, a couple who are bonding may share a ring or a bracelet as evidence that they are now going together.

Bonding also includes that period when older couples become engaged for marriage. It is as if they have felt like one for sometime and now they want to publicly announce that closeness.

Differentiating

It is interesting how many teen couples find that conflict seems to happen right after they bond. It is as if they were such good friends until they decided to go steady. This happens for a lot of reasons. However, one very predictable source of conflict and stress to a relationship as it develops is the need for the individuals to *differentiate*.

Up to this point, the couple has been doing everything that they can to emphasize their commonalities. However, as they blend, they start to feel a need to gain some distance from each other and to re-establish their own unique identity. It's all right to be viewed as Dennis-n-Paulina, or Brian-n-Christine, but sometimes partners want to be treated just as themselves and not as one-half of a relationship! Rather than emphasizing the "we," they may start to emphasize the "I" and this usually results in tension and conflict for the friendship.

Dennis, for example, may want to go out with the guys, without Paulina, or he may simply want to spend a night home with his family. Or Paulina may forget to call one night because she became involved with another friend.

Differentiation is often the point in teenage relationships that the friendship starts to dissolve. This need not be the case. Differentiation is, or should be, positive. Each person needs to see himself or herself as an individual who continues to grow and enjoy many different things. Relationships should not be so inclusive that they absorb an individual's entire life.

For many teens, a dating relationship can become overly absorbing. Dating this one person excludes all other relationships and individual forms of activity. This is not healthy. Further, when such a relationship is exclusive, it often will have a tough time surviving the differentiation stage.

Dissolution

Not all relationships continue to grow in breadth and depth. Often relationships begin to terminate or dissolve.

Even for the best of friends, the reality is that over the course of the years they will change. If each changes individually, then the relationship needs to change as well.

With this in mind it becomes obvious that many early relationships will undergo some radical changes. Most will come to an end. That doesn't mean the friendship won't continue, but the form the relationship takes will be different from what it was. Relationships change to reflect the ways the friends have changed.

Perhaps I could share a personal example. I first met my wife through her brother. He and I went to high school together and remained good friends throughout our college days. All during my high school and college days, Karen, my wife, was seen as Dave's sister. Similarly, Karen related to me as just one of her brother's friends.

Well, as it happens through high school, she and I changed. Our relationship to each other as "sister-of" and "friend-of" Dave terminated. With the termination of this earlier relationship came the opportunity to start over and *initiate* a new form of relating. We began to see each other as individuals, separate from Dave. As such, we started a new form of relating which matured and continues to mature today.

Often teens form relationships which they wish to hold onto. They will try to fix or make almost rigid their patterns of relating with one another. "We always did it this way in the past, so we will continue to do it that way!" Such relationships almost take the form of a ritual. They are not open or spontaneous but rather they are scripted, as if part of a movie or a play.

There are couples who have to call every night at seven or always go here or there on Friday or maintain some other, very predictable pattern. If they hold onto only their old patterns, the relationship is probably stagnating. Such stagnation generally marks the beginning of the end for a relationship.

A Pull toward Intimacy

As a dating relationship grows stronger, the couple typically wants to move the relationship to deeper, more personal levels (the level of intimacy).

The drive toward intimacy is very strong during adolescence. This drive, when handled appropriately, leads an individual into a fuller appreciation of who he or she is and a deeper sense of belonging.

The longer individuals date, the more time and opportunity they have to share. If they respond to this opportunity by slowly, yet progressively, opening up, their relationship will become much more intimate.

True Intimacy?

During the teen years, the experience of true intimacy may elude many adolescents. While many teens will fall in love (true love, the one and only love of their lives), the problem (not trying to be funny or sarcastic) is that people fall in true love a number of times.

The intense feelings which sometimes accompany being sexually attracted to another person are often misinterpreted as love. Yes, the feelings are enjoyable. Yes, the relationship may even be something very special. But it is not necessarily the one and only time a person will or could experience closeness with another person.

Prematurely restricting relationships to one person is a mistake. It is a mistake for one's ongoing development. It limits opportunities for personal growth, and it may lead a person to involve himself or herself in ways that he or she is not ready for nor interested in.

For example, couples who exclusively date only one another often find that their own physical attraction and strong sexual desires motivate them to experiment with sexual activity. While this desire is natural and expected, giving in to it prematurely can result in serious negative consequences (such as unwanted pregnancy) and also may lead them in directions which are contrary to God's plan.

Moreover, often when teens give in to their sexual urges they make a second mistake. In an attempt to justify or explain away their decision, they may convince themselves that their motive was (or is) true love. A few of these individuals may have found that special someone. Most, however, have simply found a sexual partner. They are mistakenly equating sexual contact with true, loving intimacy.

Relationships which are founded on sexual contact and maintained by the excitement and pleasure of that contact alone are called *pseudo-intimate* (falsely intimate) relationships. While sexual contact is intimate and certainly pleasurable, it is not, however, the sole basis upon which one can or should form a truly intimate relationship. Intimacy goes beyond physical and sexual contact. Pseudo-intimate relationships have little or no real depth or closeness, beyond physical contact.

Couples need to consider what would happen to their relationship if both parties decided never to engage in sexual contact until marriage. Would they be able to maintain a level of intimacy through nonsexual sharing? Would the relationship still be desirable? Would they still feel they're in love? If the answers to these questions are no, then perhaps the relationship is founded only on physical pleasure.

Under these conditions, the relationship is not one of sharing. It is not one of true intimacy. It really is a means of self-gratification. Is that true LOVE?

At sometime in your life, you will probably experience a relationship in which you begin to share much more of yourself. Sharing of your self, your dreams, your concerns, your history, your hopes for the future, is a sign of intimacy.

In intimate relationships, partners share their pain and their joy, their innermost selves. Sharing in this manner not only builds a relationship but moves it to a deeper more uniquely personal level. Sharing in this way is very much like the sharing and intimacy modeled by Christ.

The Gospels invite us to know the innermost person of Christ. Through prayer and openness to his response, we can experience an intimate, uniquely personal, relationship with the Lord.

In attempting to evaluate whether any relationship is appropriately and truly intimate, you need to contrast your loving relationship with that modeled by Christ. With Jesus, a loving relationship is open, not hidden or protected. With Jesus, a loving relationship encourages us to be faithful to our self, as well as to the other. With Jesus, a loving relationship is one which reflects an appropriate willingness for self-sacrifice.

With Jesus as a model of healthy, Christian intimacy, one may soon discover that the person who is pressuring another to engage in sexual contact, even though the other has shared his or her desire not to, is *self*-centered, rather than *us*-centered.

With Jesus as the model, a relationship which a person feels embarrassed about, or feels guilty about, will be recognized as nonopen and nonloving. With Christ as the model, one finds that true intimacy, true love, encourages a person to consider the other person before considering oneself.

From Saying Yes to Saying No!

Interacting and relating to another is something we all need to do. Relationships help us grow and understand more fully who we are.

To build a relationship, we need to be willing to risk and become vulnerable. We need to open up and share our private, personal self. Saying yes to sharing is a main ingredient to relationship building.

However, there are some encounters, some relationships, in which saying yes may prove personally destructive. Under these conditions, we need to learn to *say no!*

For Reflection and Discussion

- Dating can be recreation, a status symbol, an opportunity for social training, and a means of courtship. How do you see dating? How about your friends?

- Relationships develop through predictable stages. Describe what occurs during each of these stages: Initiation, Experimentation, Intensification, Integration, Differentiation (and also Dissolution).

- How would you distinguish true intimacy from pseudo-intimacy?

- With Christ as your model of love, what values do you see as essential for the experience of true love?

Chapter 8
Saying No

While he was saying this a woman from the crowd called out, "Blest is the womb that bore you and the breasts that nursed you!" "Rather," he replied, "blest are they who hear the word of God and keep it."
—Luke 11:27–28

Saying *yes* to God's word requires you to sometimes say *no* to your friends. We have heard the familiar saying: "Just Say No!" This statement can be frustrating because it seems to suggest that saying no is easy. Saying no is sometimes extremely difficult, especially when a person feels so much pressure to say yes!

Pressure Within—Needs and Drives

Physical Drives

Sexual pressure (pressure toward thinking and acting sexually) comes from many sources. One strong source of such pressure is your *physical need and drive.*

It is clear that the activation of glands and hormones results in strong desires of a sexual nature. The sometimes uncontrollable erections experienced by a teenage boy, or the romantic and erotic dreams experienced by both males and females are strong motivators to become sexually active.

Like all urges, sexual drives can be very strong. They apply much pressure and are sometimes quite hard to resist. They can, however, be controlled. They can be redirected in other ways, such as exercise or prayer.

Need for Acceptance

While the biological drive for sexual activity is strong, it may not be the strongest motivation for most teens. For many teens, sexual pressure is the result of their need to be like everyone else and to fit in (*need for acceptance*).

Other teens worry about losing their girlfriend or boyfriend if they don't become more sexually responsive. They often think: "After all, if I loved him or her, wouldn't I go all the way?"

When driven to engage in sexual activity simply as a means or a technique for being accepted, teens need to remind themselves that it is sexual activity which is being desired and needed rather than a person.

Some teens feel so isolated and so totally alone that they are willing to do whatever it takes to feel that somebody cares. Such teens need professional assistance to begin to feel more valued as a person.

One such situation can be found in case 8–1, the case of Nancy. Perhaps you know of people who have this desperate need to be accepted. These are the people who need to experience the same kind of free and unconditional love that was exemplified by Christ as he accepted Mary Magdalene. It was not because of her beauty or her sexuality that Christ loved her. Christ loved Mary Magdalene as he loves us, simply because she was (and you are) a child of God.

Case 8–1
Nancy

Nancy was a sixteen-year-old girl who had been sexually active since the age of twelve. Nancy came from a family where there wasn't much support or positive interaction. Her parents were divorced and quite often Nancy was left on her own, sometimes for days.

Being somewhat overweight, and not being able to dress like the other kids or go where the other teens went, Nancy was soon viewed as different and strange. She became somewhat of a loner. The kids would often exclude her and even make fun of the way she looked and acted.

Without the ability or the opportunity to interact with the other kids, Nancy soon began to feel very bad about herself. She developed a negative self-image and failed to develop her social skills.

Feeling isolated and totally alone, Nancy discovered that if she would allow the boys in her neighborhood to "go all the way" with her, then they would spend more time with her. Even though the boys were using her, Nancy felt—at least for short periods of time—that she was accepted and loved.

This illusion of being accepted was not at all satisfying. Her mistaken equation of sexual involvement with true acceptance and true love led to some very negative consequences. Besides failing to make her feel any better about herself, Nancy's sexual activities led to her becoming pregnant on two different occasions, for which she had abortions.

In addition, due to her bad reputation, eventually not even her sexual permissiveness would attract anybody. Everybody avoided her. No one would be seen with her. Nancy's attempts to be accepted actually led to greater rejection and isolation.

With professional help, Nancy was able to begin to develop the social skills and the self-respect she needed to reverse her destructive sexual patterns. It took some time and a lot of effort on her part but slowly she was able to begin to develop meaningful, genuine, friendships.

Need for Intimacy

Even those teens who have friends and feel like they belong are pressured to engage in sexual activity because of their own need for intimacy. Yet the reality is that, even for those seeking true intimacy, sexual contact for most teens is often anything but intimate. Early sexual activity is something which is done from a very self-serving, selfish framework and, therefore, not intimate sharing. Rather, it is simply an example of two people involved in an act of mutual use.

Rather than denying their need and interest in intimacy, teens should expand their view of intimacy beyond sexual/genital involvement. Using Christ as their model, teens can see that true intimacy involves caring, warmth, and sharing. Opening up and sharing thoughts, dreams, beliefs, and values is a wonderful way to experience intimacy.

Pressure from Outside

Pressure from Social Heroes

Saying "yes" to Christian values and "no" to the temptations of sexual activity is not easy. We live in a culture that encourages people to be free and pleasure-seeking. There are subtle messages that sex is normal, natural, and something that everybody does or should do. Many of the models or heroes, who are presented through music, television, or movies send the message that sex is cool.

Many of the heroes in the entertainment industry proudly discuss the various spouses they have had, or the people they have lived with, or the number of people with whom they currently sleep. Even some politicians and television evangelists are said to have been involved in various sex scandals.

As an exercise in recognizing this form of subtle pressure, try the following. Pretend you are a researcher from another galaxy and, therefore, know very little about our culture. As a researcher, you are trying to identify what *values* earthlings promote and live by. Your task requires you simply to observe television or listen to radio, tapes, and records for one full day. During the course of the day, write down the different references made to sex.

As you observe, keep the following questions in mind. Is sex presented as something always tied to love? Is it something which is presented as reserved for marriage? Is sex something restricted to two people committed to a relationship? As an alien visitor, do you get the feeling that sex is something special and sacred or something commonplace? How about people who promote *abstinence* (refraining from sexual intercourse)? Are they valued or are they put down and mocked?

From this day of observation, you may come to realize just how subtle yet pervasive the pressure is! Further, you may begin to realize that with such models conveying the message that it is okay to be sexually active, it is hard to say *no!*

Pressure from Friends

Perhaps one of the most pervasive pressures with which teens have to cope is the pressure from friends to be and act like them. Again, most adults would have teens think it is easy to say no to peer pressure. This *is not* the case. The pressure to conform can, under some conditions, be so great that it feels almost impossible to resist. Just consider the group pressure that was exerted on individuals in the concentration camps. The pressure was so great that many good people found themselves carrying out rules and orders which were unthinkable.

This is not to suggest that the pressure teens experience today is the same as that found in concentration camps, but extreme examples may help you appreciate that peer pressure can be very, very powerful. Resisting peer pressure takes strength of convictions as well as skills which will assist you in your resistance.

Quite often friends try to pressure one another into sexual activity by suggesting one or all of the following:

- If it feels good, do it.

- It's okay, as long as both parties agree.

- It's okay, as long as nobody gets hurt.

You need to understand that such reasoning is simply incorrect. Further, you need to know how to respond to, and reject, these attitudes.

Feeling good does not mean being good. A lot of things feel good. Just ask a heroin addict. It is clear that feelings are not the only guide nor necessarily the best guide for decision making. You need to consider the impact of your decisions on your health and well being. You need to consider what impact this act has on you physically, emotionally, psychologically, and spiritually. Your decisions need to be guided by values and principles and morals, not simply by feelings!

Agreeing doesn't make it right. While it is nice to assume that the people involved in the sexual activity mutually agree, such agreement doesn't make it right or healthy. Contrary to what some people think, the reality is: "Two wrongs *do not* make a right!"

Mutual agreement is not a sufficient guide for moral behavior. Two people can agree to do immoral, unhealthy acts.

Nobody gets hurt. A final argument sometimes used for justifying free sexual contact is that as long as nobody gets hurt, it's all right. This argument, like the others, needs to be challenged. Getting hurt is not always possible to evaluate. Having a cigarette may initially have appeared harmless, but we are coming to appreciate that smoking is anything but harmless. The reality is that neither you nor I are as skilled at looking into the future or as able to grasp the subtle and complex implications of our decisions as we may believe.

There is new and recent evidence that would suggest that early sexual activity among teens can have serious negative health consequences. Such negative health consequences, along with the possible psychological and social impact of engaging in teen sexuality, need to be considered in response to the "as long as nobody gets hurt" argument.

In addition to knowing how to reject such illogical arguments for engaging in sexual activity, teens need to feel strong enough to resist the pressure to be like everyone else. One technique is to develop a special friendship pact. This pact would be like a special agreement or promise between friends to do, or not to do, a particular thing. For example, two peers who value abstinence could help each other when in high-risk situations. They could support each other and pat each other on the back when they make those very hard, but *right* decisions to abstain. The support of just one other friend makes it easier to resist the negative group pressure.

In addition to finding such support, teens need to develop skills and attitudes which will allow them to express their feelings, opinions, and beliefs in very direct, honest, and appropriate ways (*assertiveness*). Such assertiveness will help them to say no in ways that will be heard.

Assertiveness—What Is It?

Assertiveness is the ability to express your feelings, opinions, and beliefs respectfully and firmly. Being *assertive* means that you can choose the way you wish to act in a situation rather than being limited or forced into a single way of responding. For example, suppose a group of friends went to a movie. On the way to the movie, two of the friends say, "Let's forget the movie and go get some beer!"

An unassertive person might get upset, yell, and generally act angrily and aggressively. Or a nonassertive person might become passive and allow the others to decide. An assertive person would recognize what it was that he or she wanted, and would appreciate that he or she has a right to make *his or her own decisions.*

An assertive person might say: "I feel (disappointed, concerned, irritated. . .) with your decision and I want (to go back home, to be dropped off at the movie. . .)." Directly and firmly expressing feelings and desires, without attacking another or passively surrendering, would be assertive action!

Assertive Attitude

In order to be assertive, you need to feel secure and self-confident. That doesn't mean that you have to be totally free from anxiety or nervousness. Even when you are assertive, you may feel concerned about how your friends will react to your statements. The assertive person, while concerned about the judgment of other people, will not allow that judgment and threat of evaluation from others to interfere with an honest, genuine expression of her or his own needs or beliefs.

Assertive Skills

In addition to having the right attitude, the assertive person needs to develop communication skills which help him or her express feelings and desires directly and honestly.

When asserting yourself, you want to:

1. Be honest and direct. Rather than trying to be subtle or cute or indirect, you need to say what you mean ·and mean what you say. It is important to practice being up front. This doesn't mean you need to be cruel or abusive. It does mean that you try to be specific and descriptive of how you feel, how you think. Don't hide behind humor or sarcasm or little white lies.

2. Be respectful of self and others. Being expressive and assertive means that you express your values and stand up for your right to have those values and to express them. It is important to understand that you

have a right to your opinion and the right to express it. But you also believe that others have a right to their opinion (even when it differs from yours). The assertive person expresses himself or herself while respecting the right of others to do the same.

Abstinence: A Value to Value

Saying no to premarital sexual activity is not only a communication issue, it is a value issue. In addition to learning *how* to say no, you need to value *the reasons* for saying no.

The stronger you become in your convictions that saying no and abstaining from sex have value, the easier it will become to assert that value.

Saying no makes sense for many obvious and perhaps not so obvious reasons. Table 8–1 provides some reasons often given by teens for saying no to sex.

Table 8–1
Saying No Makes Sense

Health Concerns

Sexual activity carries the obvious risks of pregnancy and sexually transmitted diseases. Premature sexual activity has additional risks. A higher rate of cervical cancer has been found in females who begin sexual intercourse at a young age and have multiple partners. A variety of other health problems are currently being studied in relation to early sexual intercourse, including the possibility of contracting a number of sexually transmitted diseases. Some of these problems are even implicated in the rising infertility rate.

Emotional and Psychological Concerns

In addition to physical risks, there are emotional risks involved in premature sexual activity. Some researchers suggest that early promiscuous sexual activity inhibits and interferes with one's ability to function sexually and emotionally later in life. For example, people engaged in early sexual activity are often reported to develop low self-esteem, feelings of inadequacy, and dependency. Such negative feelings about oneself can clearly interfere with the healthy and mature expression of love and intimacy in one's adult life.

Moral and Spiritual Concerns

Finally, in addition to the physical and emotional risks, there are social and moral risks. Christian ideals value the relational consequences of sexual activity. Our Christian tradition presents sex as belonging within the context of marriage. It is viewed as an expression of God's gift of love. It is a means of sharing that love and not an end in itself.

Premarital sexual activity runs the risk of becoming self-absorbing, self-serving, and even exploitative (taking advantage of another person, or using them). These are clearly not a reflection of the love God has for us and the love God has asked us to share.

A Model of Assertiveness

Just as we have many models who exemplify aggressive, self-serving, self-indulging sexual practices, there is one who models the ultimate in Christian assertiveness. While psychologists and mental health specialists study and research what makes for an assertive style, authors of the Bible have detailed descriptions of assertiveness—in the person of Jesus.

As you attempt to develop your own assertive skills, look to the model of Jesus for your guide. His strength of conviction, his freedom to be honest and direct in his expression of his beliefs and values, and his sensitivity and respect of the needs of others is evident throughout the Gospels. Look to Jesus. It may prove quite effective in reminding yourself to say "no" as Jesus would and "yes" as Jesus did!

For Reflection and Discussion

- Often a teen's interest in sexual activity stems from needs and pressures which are not physical in nature.

What are some nonphysical reasons some teens engage in sexual activity?

- How could you respond to someone who tries to justify engaging in sex, by stating "If it feels good, do it!" or "It's okay, if both people agree!"?

- What is assertiveness and how does it differ from aggressiveness?

- Abstinence is a worthwhile value. Abstinence makes sense for many reasons. What are some of the reasons that abstinence makes sense?

Chapter 9
New
Human Life

It was You who created my inmost self,
and put me together in my mother's womb;
for all these mysteries I thank you;
for the wonder of myself, for the wonder of your
works.
—Psalm 139:13,14

When I listen to the Gospels being read in Church, I am in total awe of the miracles performed by Christ. Awakening Lazarus from the dead, or curing a man of leprosy, is pretty powerful.

When I was younger, I used to think how neat it would be if I could see a miracle. At times, I would even get a little annoyed that God didn't seem to provide us with miracles now-a-days. Boy, was I wrong!

Can you imagine the power, the mystery, the real divine process, of having a cell from your body meet a cell from another person's body and unite. And, upon this uniting, miraculous changes occur to that one cell. It divides and increases in complexity with the ultimate creation of a real, live, human being—a human being who could be the next president or the researcher who discovers a cure for AIDS or cancer or a star athlete, pope, or super teacher. Procreation is truly a miracle.

Science can describe the unification process. It can even describe the various changes which this cell goes through in order to develop into a roly-poly, kicking, and grasping brand-new baby. Science, however, cannot explain the origin of the life force or the miracle of life.

Just as Christ raised Lazarus, so too does God breathe life into our procreated infants. The process of procreation is wondrous.

Through knowledge and understanding of the process of fetal development, you can truly appreciate and respect the power of the gift which God has given you. It is essential to understand the developmental process so that you can more fully respond to the responsibility that you will have as parents, both moms and dads, to support the ongoing development of this new life.

Conception: The Beginning

Regardless of race, creed, or nationality, and independent of your status in life, we all start out the same way. When a *sperm* unites with the egg or *ovum, conception* has occurred.

The eggs mature in the ovaries of a women. One egg is released approximately every twenty-eight days and travels down the *Fallopian tube* toward the uterus.

The eggs which provide one-half of the needed genetic material for the creation of the new life are present within a woman at the beginning of her fertile years. However, the male is continually producing new spermatozoa (sperm).

During intercourse, a male may ejaculate close to four hundred million sperm. Of the many possible combinations, only one sperm will penetrate the cell wall of the ovum during the process of conception.

The fact that only one sperm fertilizes the egg is almost magic. However, what follows next in the process of fetal development is truly unbelievable.

Prenatal Growth

The development which occurs prior to the birth of the infant is called *prenatal* (before birth). The development begins as soon as the sperm and the egg unite.

Development during this prenatal stage of life is very rapid. The new creation, this new life, will go through changes in the next nine months that take it from a tiny, single cell, to the unique, living individual of the newborn baby! The entire period of prenatal development, called the *gestation period,* usually lasts about 280 days, or nine calendar months. But not all babies decide to come out when the 280 days are up. Some may have been somewhat of a surprise early delivery (perhaps even being born prematurely). For others, the gestation period was a week or two beyond the time expected.

Talk to your parents about your own gestation period. You might ask them questions such as: How long did the pregnancy last? Was it a hard pregnancy? How did your mom and dad feel during those nine months? The answers may begin to give you a different perspective on your own development.

Gestation Period

The gestation period can be broken down into three separate periods of development called: the germinal period, the embryonic period, and the fetal period. During each of these special periods, significant changes occur, all leading to the miracle of birth.

The Germinal Period

The development which occurs during the first two weeks after conception is known as the *germinal period*. During this time, the fertilized egg begins the process of cell division that will ultimately result in the creation of a human made up of billions of cells.

Part of the miracle of life is that even though the cells of our bodies are highly differentiated based on their location and function (that is your brain cells are different than your muscle cells), the cells during our germinal period are identical. It is in the process of developing that they begin to differentiate and take on unique roles and functions.

The fertilized ovum implants itself within the mother's uterine wall. During the two weeks following conception, this fertilized egg will multiply and differentiate. By the end of this germinal period, the two-week-old fertilized egg is already well-established and ready for rapid development.

The Embryonic Period

Within four weeks after conception, the once single-cell organism now has a heart which is able to pump blood through its own veins and arteries. Just think, a tiny heart and only four weeks after conception! (Many mothers may not even realize they are pregnant.) Besides a heart, this soon-to-be new

91

baby has the beginnings of a brain, kidneys, liver, and digestive tract. There are even identifiable indentations which will become the jaws, eyes, and ears. Four weeks after conception the fetus is one-fifth of an inch long, and yet so clearly a unique, living, human being.

By the end of the embryonic period (approximately eight weeks after conception), the embryo has a uniquely human appearance. The head is clearly distinct from the body, the eyes and eyelids are taking shape; the face shows evidence of a nose, lips, tongue, and even teeth buds. After only eight weeks beyond conception, eight weeks after two single cells united, we have clear evidence of a heart beating sturdily, a brain which sends out early impulses, and a beginning organ system! Magical, perhaps not; miraculous, most definitely!

The Fetal Period

From approximately eight weeks after conception, the developing organism is called a *fetus*. Many wonderful developments occur to shape the once single-cell organism into a fully functioning, unique human being.

Within twelve weeks after conception, the fetus begins to straighten from its C-like posture. The limbs are evident, with tiny fingers and toes and even the folds for finger and toe nails. The presence of external genitals could, upon inspection, allow us to determine the sex of the fetus. The eyes are formed, the nose and the lungs have acquired shape. Yet, the fetus is still only about an ounce in weight and perhaps three inches long.

By sixteen weeks, the fetus looks like a very tiny baby. It may already have hair. All of his or her major internal organs have taken shape. Although it could not survive on its own, the development of this tiny individual has progressed to the point where all the basic systems and physical characteristics are evidenced.

From this point on, the changes come fast. The fetus continues to develop more recognizable human features, gains in weight and strength, and generally prepares for what will certainly be one of life's biggest challenges—the birth process.

The Birth Process

As the fetus completes his or her prenatal development, he or she will usually move so that his or her head is facing down in the uterus. The beginning of the birth process is not completely understood, although most researchers feel the onset of birth has something to do with the changing hormone levels in both the fetus and the mother.

When the birth process begins, the upper portion of the mother's uterus will start contracting at regular and progressively shorter time periods. This is typically known as *labor*.

Labor continues with the lower part of the mother's uterus becoming thinner and her cervix opening (*dilating*). The cervix will continue to dilate until it is approximately ten centimeters in diameter, large enough to allow the baby to exit from the birth canal into the external world.

As labor continues, the mother's abdominal muscles will begin to contract. With these contractions, the mother will begin to bear down in a process of pushing. By these rhythmic contractions and bearing down, the baby is moved through the birth canal out to the lights, sounds, and feelings of the world of a newborn.

Afterbirth

Following the birth of the infant, the mother's body will continue to contract. The uterus continues to contract and will expel the *afterbirth*. The afterbirth, is composed of the *placenta*, its membranes, and the rest of the *umbilical cord*.

Not all births proceed in the manner described. If delivery through the vagina is considered unsafe, the physician may extract the fetus by way of an incision in the mother's abdomen. This is known as a *Caesarean birth* or "C-section." Other babies may exit the vagina buttocks first. Such deliveries can be dangerous because the baby may suffocate before the head exits. This is known as a *breech birth*.

Parents as Procreators

As participants in life's miracles, parents not only share in the joy of procreation but also bear the responsibility of overseeing the healthy development of the newborn. This responsibility starts at, or perhaps even before, conception.

While the description of the developmental and birth processes appears so fixed, or preset, the reality is that there are many factors which can interfere with the normal, healthy development of a fetus. The fetus is extremely vulnerable. The earlier the stage of development, the more vulnerable the fetus is to outside influences. Even though the amniotic sac provides a relatively safe and stable environment, it is not totally immune from potentially destructive forces which can enter and alter or even kill the developing individual.

During the early part of pregnancy, the first *trimester* (first third), the developing fetus is extremely susceptible to negative environmental influences. Excessive X rays, incompatibility of the mother's blood, drugs, and poor nutrition can cause many birth defects or even death for the fetus.

Mothers

It is extremely important that a pregnant woman seek prenatal care and advice. It is important to have a proper nutritional balance. Because of the demands placed on the pregnant mother's own body, she is often prescribed supplementary vitamins.

Research also suggests that pregnant women should take as little medication as possible. The placenta, while serving as a filtration system, is less than perfect. Drugs such as heroin, alcohol, and nicotine are all known to pass through the placental wall. These drugs have been shown to create birth defects. Babies born to mothers who drink excessively have been found to have *fetal alcohol syndrome*. Some babies are born with addictions and may show signs of drug withdrawal shortly after birth (as found with mothers who were heroin addicts). Even cigarette smoking during pregnancy has been found to affect the developing fetus. Mothers who smoke may stunt the growth of their developing fetus.

Clearly, the care a woman takes of herself during pregnancy impacts on the developing fetus. A future mother is *responsible* for two lives—her own and her child's.

The influences mothers have on the developing fetus are not limited to nutrition or chemical intake. Some research is suggesting that a mother's emotional state and stress level can affect or influence the developing fetus.

Fathers

While pregnancy is always a sensitive condition, stress can be reduced if the mother finds support from those around her.

Fathering a child does not stop with conception. In fact, conception is truly just the beginning of the parenting responsibility. Since a child is created by two individuals, that child has the right and the need to be nurtured in her or his development by *two* parents.

While men have not been blessed with the gift of bearing children they can and must share in the parenting. Providing emotional support and care for the mother and developing child is essential for the healthy development of the newborn. Being supportive of the physical and emotional needs of the pregnant mother is the role and responsibility of the father.

Family

The early stages of support and communication which occur between the mother and father are the prenatal equivalents of the birth of a family. As parents share with one another the dreams, the expectations, and the concerns for their child's future, they build the connections of family. The nine months of prenatal development can, with the right care, lead to the development of not only a healthy, loving, living individual, but also a healthy, loving, and living family.

For Reflection and Discussion

- The embryonic period lasts for approximately eight weeks from conception. What are some of the unique characteristics that develop even in this brief period of time?

- What happens during the birth process? Ask about your own birth process. Was it a long labor, a difficult or easy birth?

- Why is it essential for pregnant mothers to be careful of their nutritional and chemical intake during pregnancy?

- What role can the father play during the pregnancy?

Chapter 10
Making the Heart Grow Fonder

Love is always patient and kind; it is never jealous;
love is never boastful or conceited; it is never rude or
selfish; it does not take offense, and is not resentful.
Love takes no pleasure in other people's sins but
delights in the truth; it is always ready to excuse, to
trust, to hope, and to endure whatever comes.
—I Corinthians 13:4–7

As has been suggested throughout this text, adolescence is a time of profound change. It is a time of formation. Adolescence is a time of becoming.

The emphasis of adolescence is on developing, moving, becoming, and progressing. Adolescence *is not* a time of arrival. It is not a point of completion. Adolescence is not the end or terminal stage of human development.

The reason I have emphasized this developmental process as opposed to discussing adolescence as a terminal point is because too many teens view any one experience, any one relationship, any one decision as final.

Consider Maria as an example. Maria is fifteen years old. She is a product of Catholic education, and for the past fourteen and a half years she has worked hard to follow her Christian conscience.

As a sophomore in high school, Maria fell in love. Tony was a senior at the same high school. Tony invited Maria to the homecoming dance and from that moment on it was true love, or so they thought.

True Love?

True, definitive, love can certainly happen at any time. The chances of finding and maintaining the one true love of a person's life throughout adolescence and into adult life are slim.

Since adolescence is a time of change, a time of transformation, the "you" that falls in love with the "them," will be a different "you" and "them" in the very near future. A teen's interests, wishes, and dreams—which may seem to be all-encompassing and permanently fixed—will start to change with his or her ever-changing perspective. That which seems so right now may be less appealing or attractive in the near future.

Commitments

Developing interpersonal commitments is a characteristic of the mature adult. Teens begin to experience the *capacity* for commitment, the capacity for loyalty, and the capacity for mutuality. However, like all capacities in adolescence, the capacity for commitment is still developing.

The desire and the drive toward developing intimate relationships is very strong during the teen years. It is meant to be strong. It is meant to be developing. It is meant to be cherished. Teens must be cautious, however. It is too easy for many teens to become totally absorbed by a single relationship. Prematurely locking into a relationship with one individual can restrict a person's ability for commitment and interpersonal involvement. It can prevent one from experiencing the variety of relationships needed to assist in developing the skills needed to adapt and maintain relationships.

True Love or Premature Bonding?

Although genital sexual activity during adolescence can feel good, it carries with it many potential dangers. Adolescents who engage in early genital sexual activity are at risk. Youthfulness and prematurity (physical and emotional) make teens vulnerable to being hurt by the consequences of genital activity.

Research demonstrates that early sexual activity may pressure a teen to prematurely bond. Since adolescents are in the process of developing a fuller sense of who they are, bonding (that is, making ties, or intense commitments) to another too early during development may actually interfere with a teen's identification of his or her own uniqueness.

True Love or Justification?

Quite often teens who have experienced a sexual relationship often misinterpret the basis of that relationship, convincing themselves that this is the one and only true love. True love, as reflected in the quote from Corinthians at the beginning of the chapter, requires patience, kindness, unselfishness, and it is a reflection of God, who *is* love. True love reflects the wisdom of living in accordance with God's commands—and not simply the consequence of a pleasing sexual experience.

Research suggests that most often the strong feelings of love are really part of the psychological justification for being involved in a sexual relationship.

The Sad Realities

The possibility of premature bonding and the justification that this is a true love make teens vulnerable to being hurt by the rejections which typically accompany such early bonds.

In addition to such emotional and psychological hurt, there are other practical consequences which may result from sexual activity. Besides the possibility of developing damaging reputations and experiencing the anxieties and concerns about getting caught or "doing it right," teens involved in intercourse have been found to be more vulnerable to cervical cancer and even infertility. Intercourse, especially with multiple partners, makes a teen much more vulnerable to becoming pregnant and/or contracting sexually transmitted diseases, including AIDS.

What's Needed— Knowledge!

Stating these consequences is not intended to scare or to threaten teens away from becoming sexually active. But the sad reality is that too many teens refuse to accept the fact that premature, sexual activity places a teen at risk—emotionally, socially, spiritually, and physically.

Too many teens have ideas about intercourse which are not simply wrong but which are potentially lethal. For example, you may know people who truly believe that:

- Having sex standing up, prevents pregnancy.

- Douching with water or soda after sex not only prevents pregnancy but prevents AIDS.

- Taking one birth control pill right before having sex will prevent pregnancy.

- As long as the boy withdraws his penis before he has an orgasm, the girl can't become pregnant.

- Vaginal deodorants are good forms of birth control.

These are *incorrect* beliefs and believing them can lead to some very sad consequences.

A Case for Abstinence

Our Christian tradition tells us that intercourse belongs in the committed relationship of marriage. From the perspective of our Christian tradition, sex without true and mature commitment, without fidelity, and without being open to life is outside of God's plan. In marriage, sex serves a unifying and life-giving purpose; that is, sexuality was designed by God as an expression of committed love between husband and wife and for the continuation of the human race.

Abstinence (refraining from sexual intercourse) is the *only* form of birth control which is one hundred percent effective. It is *also* the prescribed Christian standard for those outside of marriage. Abstinence not only helps people avoid the risks of pregnancy and sexually transmitted diseases, but it also reduces young people's vulnerability to premature bonding, developing a bad reputation, or being hurt by betrayal and rejection. Perhaps more than its value as a **protective** measure, abstinence is an invitation and an **opportunity** to grow in self-control, respect, and moral strength.

This opportunity for growth is available even to one who has lost his or her virginity (*i.e.*, has had sexual intercourse). Regardless of past decisions and behaviors, persons can choose to start over. They can begin to express the conviction that sexual intercourse belongs in marriage and that until then abstinence is the best choice. Such a recommitment to Christian values could be viewed as a "secondary virginity."

A Worthwhile Struggle

Many teens experience strong pressure to engage in sexual activity. The intense physical drives, extreme social pressures, and a real desire for intimacy may make their attempts to refrain from sexual intercourse (abstinence) quite difficult. The strength of these needs, these wants, may at times seem unbearable. Remaining chaste (following Christian moral standards for sexual behavior) may at times seem nearly impossible.

During these times of struggle, teens should employ the skills and the knowledge that have been presented within this program. They should recall the risks and dangers of promiscuity and should clarify their values. They should use the various techniques discussed for helping them to say "no." Most importantly, they should call out to God for support.

No one has to struggle alone. Friends, family, and God are all there for support. And following upon the model presented in Christ, who at a time of his own struggle called out to his Father to remove this cup, through prayer and an openness to a relationship with God, young persons can find the strength to respond, "Thy will be done!"

For Reflection and Discussion

- How might premature bonding (locking into an exclusive relationship before one is ready) negatively affect a teen's development?

- Often, having lost their virginity, teens may feel that it is hopeless and that they are ruined for life. How could a teen's understanding and practice of secondary virginity help?

- Think of a friendship that you have had for a number of years. How have you and your friend changed since first becoming friends? How did these changes affect your relationship?

- The chapter identified some incorrect beliefs and ideas about intercourse. What ideas have you heard (such as the one regarding having sex standing up as a means of birth control)? How are these ideas both incorrect and potentially dangerous?

Chapter 11
It Takes Two

*"But from the beginning of creation he made them
male and female. This is why a man leaves his father
and mother, and the two become one flesh. They are
no longer two, therefore, but one flesh. So then, what
God has united, human beings must not divide."*
—Mark 10:6–9

I can remember the day as if it were yesterday. My wife
Karen was a senior in college. I was at work as a teacher in a
Catholic high school. I had a break between classes and I went
to the main office to use the phone.

Karen had been feeling pretty sick for the last couple of days
and her doctor wanted to take some tests. I was nervous when
I called; we were newlyweds, just married a month, and I was
concerned about her.

I called the doctor and I can still hear him say,
"Congratulations, Mr. Parsons, you are going to be a father!"

Hearing the doctor's words of congratulations and realizing
that my wife was pregnant created a wave of emotion which
seemed to flood over me. Initially, I was filled with excitement
and joy over the thought of becoming a parent. But excitement
and joy were soon replaced by concern and anxiety.

After all, I was a teacher; Karen was still a student. How
were we to afford a child? I even became somewhat selfish,
thinking, this isn't how *we* planned it. We were supposed to
save and buy a house. We were supposed to enjoy being
newlyweds for awhile and *then* we would settle down to raise
a family. Somehow our plans and God's plans didn't
completely mesh.

A Life-Changing Experience

Having a baby certainly transforms a parent's life! Many of the dreams a person had will either have to be deferred or forgotten. Swamped with responsibilities that a new parent most likely doesn't know how to handle, one finds that life has been drastically changed.

When I think of how scary it was in the beginning for us as about-to-be parents, my heart goes out to those many teenage parents who are even less prepared than we were. I was twenty-four years old, with a college degree and a stable job, and married. My wife was finishing her college degree. We had some savings in the bank and a good health insurance plan. Yet, with all of these supports, the experience of knowing we were about to be responsible for the life of another human being was very scary.

If it was that stressful for us, then what must it be for those teens who are much less prepared to meet the demands, financially, emotionally, and physically, than we were? Yet many teenagers this year, this month, this day, will be hearing that same message: "You are going to be parents!"

A Gift, A Joy—Not Easily Received

Teenage pregnancy happens. It happens to approximately one out of every ten girls a year. It can happen regardless of who you are, where you live, or how much education or money you have.

The miracle of pregnancy is a gift from God. The true wonder of the developing fetus and the experience of a laughing, curious newborn are meant to be experiences to be enjoyed. Too often, however, the stress of pregnancy for the ill-prepared teenage parents overshadows the gift and the joy which is meant to be there! The risks, the struggles, the negatives of an unwanted or ill-prepared pregnancy too often feed on themselves and start a vicious downward spiral for parent and child.

So Many Risks

Risks to Health

Teenage girls who have babies run more health risks than women in their twenties. The younger the girl, the more such health risks become an issue, not just for the teenager but also for her baby.

Research has demonstrated that babies born to young mothers often have more medical problems than do those born to women in their twenties. Problems, such as malnutrition, toxemia, hypertension, prolonged labor, and complications in delivery, seem to be more frequent with teenage mothers. In cases where mothers have not yet completed their own physical development, for example with mothers under fifteen, these health problems are even more likely.

Further, the younger the mother, the more likely that the baby will be born prematurely. Premature infants of low birth weight and added medical complications may result in children who have developmental problems. Such developmental problems increase the responsibilities placed upon these young parents.

The risk of severe neurological impairment or lower capacity to resist infection are also significantly higher for babies born to teenage mothers.

In addition to the health risks to the pregnant mother and fetus, research demonstrates that the risks to the child continue after birth if the teenage parents do not receive the support they need.

Risk of Abuse

The frustrations experienced during the early years of parenting are compounded by the teen's lack of understanding, limited maturity and ability to cope with stress, limited resources and support. This frustration often leads to infant neglect and/or abuse. Extreme spanking, shaking, or punishing, in response to the frustrations of not being able to quiet their crying infant, is all too familiar and all too devastating.

Education and Employment Risks

Most of the research would suggest that teenagers who become pregnant do not marry and do not place their infants up for adoption. Even for those who do marry, the results are often the same.

The mother and father are forced to withdraw from school so that they can care for the baby and/or seek full-time employment. Without a high school education, teenage parents are more likely to end up on welfare and in low-paying, nonadvancing positions.

There are always success stories and exceptions to the rule. But teens must be cautious not to gloss over the realities. Yes, perhaps some teens are able to continue their education; someone might even find a lucrative job, but the chances are very small.

Social Risks

At a time when peers and social activities are so important, teenage pregnancy forces the young mother and father from the mainstream of peer activity. Somehow, going to the prom or out to the dance just doesn't seem to work as well when you are eight months pregnant or when you are struggling to make enough money to buy diapers.

Initially, a teenager's pregnancy may be somewhat of a novelty to her friends. The father-to-be may even find some of his buddies praising him and supporting him. The reality is that the novelty and the support wears thin very rapidly. For most teens, finding their own ways, making their own relationships, expanding their own friendships, and enjoying the freedom of their teen years are what is important. Being with teenage parents restricts their freedom.

The events of a teenage parent's day and the things that concern them are not of interest to most of their old friends. They may want to keep the relationships going, but by definition the teenage parent is different now. The teenage mom and dad have crossed into the responsibilities of adulthood and their old friends have not. Slowly, but surely, being teenage parents restricts social contacts and may isolate the new parents from their friends of old.

Emotional Risks

Suicide among teenage mothers is much higher than for the general public. The pressures and responsibilities of parenthood are great. These pressures are compounded by the fact that teenage parents don't have the knowledge, skills, or resources to meet many of the demands they experience.

The pressure and emotional strain is increased by the fact that many teenage parents experience social pressure to abort the child or place their baby up for adoption. Often, there is the feeling of social embarrassment. The pregnant girl may be treated as an outcast or as a shame and embarrassment to her family and friends.

Even if the teenage parents survive the pregnancy and delivery and decide to keep the child, the emotional pressures are just beginning. The normal frustrations of parenting are compounded by the limited financial resources, the inability to communicate and share responsibilities with each other, or the limited emotional development of the teenage parent. The statistics on the frequency of abandonment, suicide, alcoholism, and child abuse all provide testimony to the stress and emotional distress experienced by many teenage parents.

With All of These Risks, Then Why?

Given the grim realities of teenage pregnancy and teenage parenting experiences, the question could be asked, "Why do teens become pregnant?"

What may seem to be a simple and straightforward question is really a lot more complicated than it seems at first. While teenagers cite a number of reasons for becoming pregnant—"It was an accident," "I love her," "I thought it would be neat," "I thought that it would keep him with me forever"—the deeper explanations may be placed in four general categories. Teenage pregnancy most often seems to be the result of: *Misinformation, Immaturity, Insecurity, Low Self-Esteem.*

Misinformation: It Can't Happen to Us!

Many teenagers who find that they are pregnant or that they have fathered a child report that they simply didn't think it could happen to them. Often their failure to recognize the connection between pregnancy and sex stems from a number of misconceptions.

It may seem silly or almost unbelievable, but I have had teens tell me that they were surprised that they got pregnant or that they got their girlfriend pregnant since:

- "We made love standing up."

- "Every time we had sex she would wash her genitals with Pepsi."

- "I never came (ejaculated) within her."

Many teens lack accurate information about the biology of intercourse and conception. Many think that pregnancy can be prevented if they make love only once or only in a certain position. Many teens believe that conception can be prevented after intercourse, if the girl and/or even the boy wash their genitals with soda or vinegar.

But probably one of the most widely held misconceptions involves the belief that if the boy withdraws his penis prior to ejaculation, the girl will not become pregnant. The problem with this reasoning is that all too often in the excitement and pleasure of the moment the boy will not be ready nor willing to withdraw and, thus, many accidents of ejaculation within the vagina occur. Further, most teenagers fail to realize that even before ejaculation, the male secretes semen containing sperm. All it takes is one sperm to impregnate the awaiting egg.

Teens need to remember that the *only* sure form of birth control is *abstinence!*

Immaturity: A Baby Is Neat!

Some teenage boys and teenage girls think that having a baby would be neat. Being a parent can definitely be a neat experience, however, too many teens equate having a baby with having a pet or a toy.

Many times, pregnant teens will state that they wanted something to share. For some teens, having a baby is equated with sharing a ring or a gift.

The emotional immaturity of some teens prevents them from truly seeing the larger picture. They are unable to appreciate the responsibility that parents are given. When you are a parent, you are *responsible for another human being's life!* Somehow, "neat" just doesn't express it.

A young baby requires a huge amount of patience, time, and commitment. Babies need to be waited on for all of their needs. You can not simply put them away as if they were toys, only to be taken off the shelf later and played with.

To emphasize the awesomeness of this responsibility, consider interviewing your own parents about their experience with pregnancy. How did it affect them? What are the joys they received? What are the concerns and fears? How did having children open new doors of experiences and opportunities? Also, how did having children change their life-styles and restrict their previous freedoms?

The goal of such an interview is not to cast parenting into a light of negativity. Far from it! Talking with mature, responsible parents should help you appreciate the real gift of parenting and respect the awesome responsibility it entails.

Insecurity

For some teens, getting pregnant is a way of securing a relationship. For many teens who are unsure and insecure about the love of their partner, becoming pregnant or getting her pregnant is falsely viewed as a means of making him or her stay.

The problems with such an orientation are evident. If your love is one in which your partner needs to be trapped, then it is not love. Getting one pregnant or becoming pregnant yourself is not a guarantee that your partner will stay in the relationship. And if they do stay in a relationship because of pregnancy, it will be with such resentment and anger that you probably will not want them around.

Teens who feel a desperate need to trap their partner in a relationship need to step back and consider the following.

- My partner doesn't need to trap me, so if it is love, and if it is mutual, why do I need to trap him or her?

- Being forced to do something I don't want to do makes me furious. Do I really want a partner for life who may be furious at me because I forced him or her into it?

- What happens to me if my plan fails and my partner still leaves me?

- What about the baby? Do I really want to use another person's *life* as a tool to emotionally bribe my partner?

Those teens who feel so desperate and anxious about being alone and are unable to see the negatives of such entrapment might be demonstrating extremely low self-esteem and should consider seeking professional assistance.

Low Self-Esteem

Often pregnancy is viewed as a means for establishing a teen's worth as a person. For many teens with low self-esteem, low sense of worthwhileness, having a baby is seen as evidence that they are grown up and mature. It is viewed as evidence of their manhood or womanhood and, therefore, as evidence of their personal value.

Teens with such low self-esteem use pregnancy as a vehicle for feeling that they are loved. For some teens, the need to love and to be loved in return is so strong that the risks of teenage pregnancy seem insignificant. For these teens with such a fragile sense of their own self-worth and their own lovableness, pregnancy and a baby to love appear to be the answer.

While there is no simple solution to the problem of low self-esteem, we know that pregnancy is *not* the answer. Our discussion in chapter 1 on the factors affecting self-esteem would suggest that becoming a teenage parent would most likely threaten a person's self-esteem rather than raise it. Teenage parents generally experience a lowering of their sense of personal *competence, power, virtue,* and *significance.* Thus, most teenage parents experience, at least initially, a lowering of their self-esteem.

Teens who approach pregnancy and teen parenting as a solution to their own limited sense of worth, need the support of their friends and family. They also need professional assistance.

But, I Am Pregnant— So Now What?

Even when teens understand the various facts and figures about teenage pregnancy and even though they have Christian values, the reality is that some may become pregnant. The evidence is clear. There is more information being given to teens and yet, out-of-wedlock pregnancies continue to occur—and with tragic outcomes.

Teens who are pregnant or have gotten their partner pregnant must make a number of decisions. These decisions are essential. They will impact the young woman's life, the young man's life, and the life of their offspring.

Pregnancy is not a one-person responsibility. As the quote from Saint Mark at the beginning of the chapter noted, *"They are no longer two, therefore, but one flesh."* Both man and woman shared equally in the impregnation and now need to share equally in promoting the healthy development of the child. They will need much support. There are health and prenatal concerns for which they will need guidance. There are emotional issues which need to be addressed. There are decisions regarding the way they will choose to respond to this pregnancy, which they will have to make. All of these decisions are tough. There is no easy answer. Hopefully, they will find the support they need in their partner, their family, their community, and their Church.

In the next chapter we will discuss a number of the options which a pregnant teen needs to consider.

For Reflection and Discussion

- Think about your plans for next year. Think about your summer vacation, what you want to do, anything you may want to get, or places you may want to go. Think about how you spent your time over the last two weeks. Now imagine that you are a parent. How might your long-term plans and even your day-to-day activities change?

- Teen pregnancy is risky. What type of risks do teen mothers and their babies face?

- How does each of the following, misinformation, immaturity, insecurity, and low self-esteem, contribute to teen pregnancy?

- Imagine your friend just told you that she (or another friend) is pregnant. What would you suggest she do, immediately? Why?

Chapter 12
There Is
No Easy
Answer

"Let the children come to me and do not hinder them.
It is to just such as these that the kingdom of God
belongs. I assure you that whoever does not accept
the reign of God like a little child shall not take part
in it." Then he embraced them and blessed them,
placing his hands on them.
—Mark 10:14–16

As noted in the previous chapter, hearing the words: "You are going to be a parent!" places teens in a position of having to make many very difficult decisions. Making the correct, responsible decisions during this time will be the most difficult thing they have ever had to do.

In chapter 6, we discussed a general model or guide for decision making. That model suggested that, in making a major decision, you should:

- Identify the problem and what you hope to achieve.

- Delay your immediate impulsive response.

- Find a variety of paths or solutions.

- Evaluate each possible path for consequences.

- Select and make your decision.

This model needs to be employed to make a responsible, value-based decision regarding pregnancy.

A Decision to Be Shared

Becoming pregnant required the participation of both the boy and the girl. Making decisions in response to a pregnancy is an activity which also needs to be shared by both the boy and the girl.

It may seem like an unbearable task, but the first decision to make is to share the fact of the pregnancy with one's partner and one's parents. This is a time during which thoughts will be clouded and confused and emotions will be running very high. It is important to seek and find support from those who may be able to approach this situation with both love and a calmer, more objective perspective.

A Decision Requiring Clear Thinking

When initially confronted by the reality of pregnancy, teens may often panic. They may feel that their lives are over or that the pregnancy is a real catastrophe. If they are to make the best possible decision, they will need to have an accurate and realistic sense of the problem. For most teens, emotions are so elevated that the problem, while being very serious, is considered much worse, much more catastrophic than it has to be.

Emotional reactions to events, whether the event is positive or negative, is actually caused not by the event being experienced (for example, being pregnant), but by the interpretation or meaning given to the event. For example, think about a little child who is terrified of the dark. If you really think about what is causing the feeling of terror, you will most likely see that it is *not* the dark (the event) which causes this child's terror. What is causing the emotional reaction of fear for this child is his or her own thinking process. The child starts to think that there is a monster in the dark. Once he or she believes that there is a monster, then the child reacts to that belief, to that interpretation, as if it were true. The terror felt is real. The point is that this terror is caused by a mistaken belief in the existence of the monster and not by the reality of only a darkened room.

Extreme emotional reactions are similarly caused by a person's interpretations or "mis-interpretations." The feelings are a result of the beliefs or the meanings given to certain events. Thus, teens who feel overwhelmed by the news of their upcoming parenthood may feel so because of their exaggerated interpretation of the impact of this situation.

If they quieted themselves and listened to the way they interpret what is happening, they may hear themselves talking inside their heads. Their self-talk may be saying things such as: "My life is over!" "I'm dead!" "This is the worst thing that could ever happen!" "I'll never be able to face my family, my friends!"—or some other similarly extreme and devastating interpretation. Even though becoming a parent certainly has a significant impact on one's life, life is not, nor need it be, over!

The first step is to start arguing with this type of thinking. At this time of emotional crisis, one needs to slow down and attempt to gain a rational perspective. Yes, it is true that this is something very serious. It is true that life is about to undergo major changes. What is *not true* is that life is over or ruined. Teens need to view this situation as a real and serious problem. It is *not*, however, a catastrophe and must not be treated as one.

In order to decatastrophize the situation (reduce the catastrophe back to the level of a serious problem), the persons involved must identify exactly what the pregnancy does mean and how it will, *in fact*, affect their lives, the life of those around them, and the life of the baby. It may help the couple to actually sit down and begin to make a list of the expected impacts due to the pregnancy. But before they list one of the consequences, they should be sure that it can be actually proven true.

A Decision Requiring Knowledge

Hard choices require clear, rational thinking. They also require some understanding about the possible alternatives available to you. In order to make a responsible decision, a person needs to know the options available and the consequence of each of these options.

Catholic teenagers need to know that one option, abortion, does not have the approval of the Church community. Abortion is a willful act ending the life of a fetus by removing the fetus from the uterus. Church teaching and tradition hold that human life exists and must be protected and nourished from the moment of conception. Thus, the life conceived has the same right to live and thrive as any other life. Saint Mark tells us that Jesus "embraced them (the children) and blessed them." Every child's life is embraced and blessed by the Lord. Decisions regarding pregnancy must reflect a similar loving and embracing.

The other options—teen marriage, single parenting, and adoption—are not easy solutions. Each of these options has advantages and disadvantages. Each of these options needs to be carefully considered and discussed before a decision is made.

As part of the decision-making process, one needs to objectively consider each of the options available, gather information about the process involved in each option, and identify the various advantages and disadvantages of each.

Some of the arguments for and against each of the options available are listed in the following section. This is certainly not an exhaustive list. Each of these options should be discussed with one's partner. It may also help to share perspectives with one's parents or with a professional counselor. Their distance from the problem may help them be a bit more objective. They may act as a rational counterbalance to the couple's own emotional perspective.

Choices: Reasons For and Against

Marriage

Teen marriages appear to be on the upswing. There are various reasons teens choose marriage in response to being pregnant, and many reasons some teens choose not to marry. (See table 12–1.)

Table 12–1
Marriage and Parenthood

Why Some Choose It	Why Some Do Not Choose It
• think the baby should live with two parents	• aware of the high divorce rate for teenage marriages
• love the other person—had planned to get married anyway	• know they are too young for marriage
• believe they are ready for a permanent, committed relationship	• partner does not want to marry or is not seriously committed to the other
• believe it is the only "right" way to keep the baby (if married)	• does not think partner would make a good parent or spouse
• want the baby to "have a name"	• believe they are not ready to marry, do not love their partner, are not committed to each other
• are pressured by parents, boyfriend, girlfriend, or peers	• think they have sufficient support from family or other sources to raise baby alone
• are looking for financial support or sharing of parenting responsibilities	• are pressured not to get married

Rev. John E. Forliti. *Valuing Values: Program Manual* (Dubuque, Iowa: BROWN Publishing–ROA Media, 1986).

Most of the statistics point to the fact that teen parents who marry in response to pregnancy often divorce in the end. The divorce rate for those married in their teens is three to four times higher than for any other age group.

Deciding to marry because of pregnancy is not a wise decision. It is a better idea to separate the questions: "What to do with the baby?" and "Should we get married?" Then make two distinct decisions about those two issues. Attempting to avoid embarrassment or wanting to give the baby a name are simply not good reasons to make a commitment for life in marriage.

This is not to suggest that such teen marriages can't work. Some do, but they are the exceptions to the rule. Teen marriages require a lot of support from others and very real effort on the part of the teens.

Teens contemplating marriage should consider prenuptial counseling by a professional counselor. Such prenuptial counseling can assist the couple in discussing issues such as sexuality, children, money, household duties, careers, and so forth. Further, through such prenuptial counseling, the couple can learn needed communication skills which will help them work through the many problems and decisions confronting a young married couple.

It is also a good idea for teens who are married to continue with their supportive counseling throughout the first year of marriage. Through counseling, the couple can find the support and tools they need to assist them through the various trouble spots of the first year of marriage.

Single Parenting

Over fifty percent of pregnant teens choose to remain single, at least for a time, and raise the baby as single parents. Raising a child as a single-parent teenager is extremely difficult.

For most of these single-parent teens, life becomes marked by repeated pregnancies, unstable family life, and welfare dependency. Being a single mother and a teenager at the same time can present several real hazards. In addition to being forced to quit school, most teenage mothers find it difficult to find adequate career training. The pressure of raising a child, along with a sense of being isolated from the rest of her teenage friends and unable to experience the fullness of her adolescent years, may make a teenage mother vulnerable to engaging in child abuse. Raising a baby as a single teen mother is very difficult. It is not impossible, however.

For the teen wishing to become a single parent, support from her family and from the father of the child becomes essential. In addition to the financial support she will need, the single teen mother will need emotional and social support as well. She will need time away from the baby. She will need time and energy to pursue her education or to gain employment. She will need the opportunity to develop new friendships and/or maintain the old ones. And in each of these situations, she will need someone to care for the baby in her absence, however brief.

In addition to such baby-sitting and financial assistance, a teen single parent will need to have a person to whom she can turn when feeling unsure or insecure about her parenting. She needs to feel that her own parents will be there to support her and to share their experience and expertise.

Perhaps the thing most needed by the teen mother is clarity and vision. She needs to truly understand her motives for keeping the child. She needs to be sure that it is love for the child and not some personal, selfish need which motivates her.

Often such love for the child, and true concern for the child's well being, may lead the mother to understand that placing the baby for adoption is the best and most loving thing to do.

Adoption

Separating from a baby who has been part of her very being for the past nine months of pregnancy is not an easy task for most women. Placing a child up for adoption requires extreme love and vision on the part of the teenage parents. There can be many reasons that a teen would choose to place their child for adoption, and some reasons why they may not. (See table 12–2.)

Table 12–2
Adoption

Why Some Choose It	Why Some Do Not Choose It
• not ready to be a parent	• believe adoption is wrong, that a person should not let go of something that is part of them
• feel pressure from boyfriend, girlfriend, family, or peers to place baby for adoption	• feel pressure from parents, friends, boyfriend, girlfriend, community to keep the baby
• want more for the baby than they are able to provide; want baby to have two parents	• want to have and keep the baby because: a. it is part of them b. it is their responsibility since they became pregnant
• are unable to support or care for an infant financially or in other ways	c. they want someone to love d they feel they are ready to take on the responsibilities of parenthood
• are unwilling to have an abortion, and not ready to choose parenting	• may not be placed in a good home
• want to finish school, go on to college, realize personal life goals	• do not know much about adoption or its availability

Rev. John E. Forliti. *Valuing Values: Program Manual* (Dubuque, Iowa: BROWN Publishing–ROA Media, 1986).

Teenage parents who choose to place their baby up for adoption recognize that it is the baby's best interest that motivates them to make such a decision.

Such a decision, while perhaps the best one, can be quite painful. Teens who choose adoption often experience real grief and bereave their loss. These teens are entitled to their grief. It is a significant loss they have experienced. Yet, they need to be reminded of the real love demonstrated in their decision.

Providing their child with the best opportunity for healthy development, with a family who is able and willing to nurture them, is truly an act of sacrifice and love.

Teens who are unable to find comfort in knowing that what was done is best for the child may need professional support and counseling.

No Easy Answer

Hearing the positive pregnancy test result and following this news with responsible decisions and behaviors is one of the most difficult set of choices a teen will ever make. While the choices available can be clearly identified, the choosing is far from easy.

Teens confronted with this decision need to understand the choices available and how each choice affects those many people who are involved—the teen mother, the teen father, the baby, and the families of the teenagers. With knowledge of the options available, an ability to use a good decision-making model, the support of a loving family, and the grace of God, teens can make those decisions, those choices, which are ultimately best for them and their child.

For Reflection and Discussion

- Teens who become pregnant need to be aware of the various options open to them. What are the pros and cons for selecting each of the following?

  - Teenage marriage

  - Single parenting

  - Adoption

- What might be some of the thoughts and feelings which emerge as a teen tries to decide between the options of teenage marriage, single parenting, or adoption?

Chapter 13
Staying Healthy

"Be compassionate, as your Father is compassionate. Do not judge, and you will not be judged. Do not condemn, and you will not be condemned. Pardon, and you shall be pardoned."
—Luke 6:36–37

Tom is fifteen. Julie is an honors student who comes from a very wealthy, Christian family. Henry is only thirteen, a runaway. Then there are Janet, Rico, Jason, Jose, and Rakita. The list goes on—teens with varied backgrounds. Some are rich; others quite poor. Many come from good, two-parent homes; some have no home at all. So many different backgrounds and experiences yet each share one thing in common. They are all infected with a sexually transmitted disease (STD).

People who have contracted a form of sexually transmitted disease do not need to be judged or condemned. They need to experience our compassion as the Father is compassionate. In order to be compassionate, and to be safe, young Christians need an understanding of the what and why of sexually transmitted disease and to order their lives according to their Christian values.

Sexually transmitted disease (STD) does not discriminate between men and women, young and old, rich and poor. It doesn't favor one race or nationality. It is a threat to all who are sexually active.

While the statistics will vary, it can be safely assumed that STD claims over 500,000 new victims each year between the ages of fifteen and twenty-four. This staggering number refers only to those cases of STD which are reported and treated. This does not account for the thousands which go unreported and untreated!

The concern regarding the devastating and epidemic impact that STD has had on our nation has become even more significant with the inclusion of AIDS among the growing list of sexually transmitted diseases (STDs).

The purpose of this chapter is to increase your awareness and sensitivity to the serious consequences of sexual activity. It is not intended to be a medical exposition of every symptom, cause, and treatment for all of the sexually transmitted diseases.

It is essential to understand the nature of this group of diseases. It is essential to dispel the false notions, such as: "Nice people can't get STDs" or "If you have sex only once, you will not get STDs."

Sexually transmitted diseases are contracted by very nice people. STDs can be contracted after only *one* sexual encounter. STDs can be contracted anytime someone's genitals, rectum, or mouth comes in contact with the genitals, rectum, or mouth of someone already infected. Sexually transmitted diseases **are not selective!**

Why an Epidemic?

Why are sexually transmitted diseases increasing so rapidly among young people? One reason is simply a matter of numbers. There are more young people today than ever before. But this is not the total reason.

Sexually Active

It is clear, through a variety of attitudinal surveys and the increasing number of teen pregnancies, that teens today are more sexually active than those of yesterday. Further, it is clear that as the frequency of sexual contact and the number of varied partners increases so do the chances of contracting a sexually transmitted disease.

Ignorance and Naivete

In addition to increased sexual activity, many teens are simply ignorant of the facts about STDs and the measures to be taken to avoid contracting them. Even among those teens who know the facts, there are many who naively believe that they won't contract STDs. It simply won't happen to them. Being indifferent to the dangers of STDs or being embarrassed about employing techniques to avoid contraction of STDs is not only stupid, but *potentially fatal!*

Knowledge—The First Step

The first step required is to gain solid, accurate information about the various forms of STDs, their symptoms, their causes, and the steps needed for prevention and treatment.

STDs—What We Know

Sexually transmitted diseases are very serious. They are not only highly contagious but also can be physically debilitating and, in some cases, *fatal.* Although there are many types of sexually transmitted diseases, four are especially frightening and can cause irreparable damage or death. These four, Gonorrhea, Syphilis, Herpes, and AIDS, are discussed below.

Gonorrhea

Gonorrhea is caused by gonococcus bacterium. It usually shows up in men two to six days after sexual contact with a person who has it; however, it sometimes doesn't show up for a month or more. The symptoms a man will have include pus dripping from the penis or a burning feeling while urinating. However, about ten percent of the men who contract gonorrhea will have no symptoms at all and will continue to spread the disease to anyone with whom they have sex. A woman may experience a slight vaginal discharge with a burning feeling; however, most of the time there are no symptoms at all. This is one of the reasons why it is extremely important for an infected person to inform his or her sexual partner so they can be treated and not unknowingly spread the disease to others. Gonorrhea can only be diagnosed and treated by a medical professional. An examination, smear, and culture are necessary. (Culture: a sample is put on a special gel surface called an agar plate and allowed to grow for a few days.) If gonorrhea is identified, the usual treatment includes two injections of penicillin. Gonorrhea that is untreated can cause sterility, arthritis, heart trouble, and general bad health. A complication of gonorrhea in women can include pelvic inflammatory disease (PID) which is a painful disease of the pelvic organs, often causing fever. It can result in sterility. Sterility is caused by scar tissue that blocks the fallopian tubes. Approximately fifty thousand women a year become sterile because of gonorrhea. In men, sterility can result from scar tissue causing blockage of the vas deferens. If a mother has gonorrhea at the time of delivery, the infant is at risk of blindness if the infant's eyes are not medicated.

Syphilis

Syphilis is caused by a spirochete bacterium. The first sign of syphilis is usually a sore, called a chancre. In men, it usually appears on the penis and in women it usually occurs inside the vagina. The chancre at first may look like a pimple or wart. It gradually becomes larger and is usually painless. Chancres can also appear on the mouth or breasts. They sometimes cause swelling of the lymph nodes in the groin and are extremely infectious. They usually disappear in three to six weeks. At the time the chancres occur, if syphilis is undetected or untreated, the disease will develop into stage two. Stage two usually comes a month to six months after the first stage has disappeared and commonly lasts for six weeks to six months. The most common symptoms are like those of the flu—fatigue, aching joints and muscles, and fever. Other symptoms can include a painless rash often seen on the palms of the hands or soles of the feet, swollen lymph nodes, and hair loss in patches. After stage two, if untreated, latent stage or stage three will develop. During stage three, the disease enters a silent stage. During this time, the syphilis travels throughout the body and can cause damage, often permanent, to various organs of the body. This stage can last from one to twenty years. Syphilis can be diagnosed with a simple blood test and treated with antibiotic therapy. If treated during stages one or two, there are no complications. However, if it is allowed to enter stage three, the complications are very serious: brain damage, heart and blood vessel disease, kidney disease, and possible death from any of these. If a mother is pregnant and the infant becomes infected, serious damage and disfigurement may result, including death. For this reason, many states require blood tests for syphilis before a couple can marry, and pregnant women are tested soon after becoming pregnant so that if the test is positive, treatment can be given immediately.

Herpes

Herpes is caused by the herpesvirus and is often mistaken for syphilis. In recent years, herpes has become more common and has now reached epidemic proportions in the United States. Groups of painful blisters appear on the sex organs or pubic area. The sores look somewhat like fever blisters or cold sores on the lips but are caused by a different virus. The sores are extremely painful and may last between seven and twenty-eight days. The sores will go away. However, the disease does not. It can occur over and over again. Stress has been linked as a cause for reoccurrence. Women who have herpes are advised to have pap smears on a regular basis for the rest of their lives, because a woman's chance of having an abnormal pap smear is higher after she has had herpes. If a pregnant woman has herpes at the time she is due to give birth, the infant can contract the disease passing through the birth canal. Herpes is very dangerous to a newborn infant and can cause permanent damage to the central nervous system and sometimes death. If a pregnant woman has active herpes or suspects she may have herpes at the time of delivery, a caesarean section will be performed. It is extremely important for anyone who has herpes to inform their partner and to avoid any sexual contact during active outbreaks.[1]

AIDS

One of the most devastating of all STDs is AIDS. The Acquired Immune Deficiency Syndrome (AIDS) is a disease which, as of this writing, is still not well understood. New information regarding the pattern of this disease, the possible agents involved in creating the disease, and the approach to treatment is still under investigation.

Acquired Immune Deficiency Syndrome (AIDS) appears to be caused by a virus called HIV (Human Immunodeficiency Virus). Not everyone who is infected with HIV gets AIDS. Some ten to thirty-five percent of the people infected with HIV will develop AIDS; another twenty to twenty-five percent will develop ARC (AIDS Related Complex). Some people with ARC become very sick while others have only minor illness. A very serious concern for health officials is that some forty percent or more of the people infected with HIV remain symptom-free. They often do not know they are infected and can be transmitters of the virus to others.

Medical researchers have developed a test to detect antibodies to the HTLV-III virus in the blood. It's hoped that use of this test will ensure the safety of the nation's blood supply and make early treatment possible. To date, there is no

1. The paragraphs on Gonorrhea, Syphilis, and Herpes are from *Valuing Values: Program Manual* by Rev. John E. Forliti (Dubuque, Iowa: BROWN Publishing–ROA Media, 1986).

cure for AIDS, but medical research has discovered that the use of radiation, surgery, and drugs such as Interferon, can be used to treat some of the illness associated with AIDS.

We know that AIDS is *not* transmitted by ordinary, nonsexual contact such as touching. AIDS is a disease that is transmitted through high-risk activities. These high-risk activities include sexual activity with someone who is infected with AIDS and intravenous drug use. Sadly, we now know that AIDS can also be passed on from an infected mother to her baby during pregnancy or at the time of birth.

The symptoms of AIDS aren't always clear. And since the incubation period of AIDS may range from a few months to years, the symptoms may not show up for some time. People with AIDS often report extreme fatigue, loss of appetite, extreme weight loss, swollen lymph glands all over their body, night sweats, and skin infections which do not heal. Most people who contract AIDS die within two to four years.

Other Forms of STDs

While these are clearly the most devastating of the sexually transmitted diseases, there are others. Each disease has different symptoms. Some men and women will not get any symptoms at all. They act as carriers of the disease, passing it on without even knowing they have it. Table 13–1 lists additional information about these specific diseases. The goal of the chapter is not to make you medically proficient or experts in STDs. But you must be aware and knowledgeable!

Review this list, discuss it with your teacher, your friends, your parents, and the person you are dating.

Loving yourself and loving another demands that you become sensitive to these real threats to your health, the health of your partner, and ultimately the health of our society.

Reducing the Chances

Clearly, the best and surest way to protect oneself from contracting a sexually transmitted disease is to not have sex. Abstinence is both the best preventive method and the only one morally acceptable to Catholics. However, people who are sexually active can reduce their chances of contracting STDs by not having sex with multiple partners. The chances can also be lessened through use of a condom.

Many people who have contracted STDs don't know they have the disease nor do they show immediate symptoms. Further, many who do know they have STDs remain dishonest and do not inform their partner. It must be emphasized that the responsibility for protection rests with oneself and not one's partner.

But What If...?

Symptoms of a sexually transmitted disease include:

- sores (around the genitals)

- discharge (such as drip or flow from the genitals)

- burning urination

- itching (around the genitals)

- warts (around the genitals)

- pain in the lower abdomen or groin

These symptoms are not to be ignored or wished away. Persons who suspect exposure to STDs need to seek help at once. They need to consult a family physician, a local public health center, or a hospital outpatient clinic—for examination, testing, and treatment if needed.

Since some of the STDs are symptom-free (not showing any of the listed signs), it may be a good idea for sexually active teens to seek blood and culture tests whenever they have regular physical examinations.

Persons who have a sexually transmitted disease must tell their partner(s) so that they can also receive proper treatment. Moreover, persons under treatment for STD must stop having sex *until the disease is cured*—not just until the symptoms go away.

Table 13–1
Sexually Transmitted Diseases (STDs)

Name	Facts
Gonorrhea	Treatable with penicillin. Most women and some men have NO symptoms. Spread only by sexual contact.
Herpes	Caused by herpes 2 virus. Has reached epidemic proportions in the United States. There is treatment but NO cure at this time.
Syphilis	Treatable with penicillin, antibiotics. Spread only by sexual contact.
AIDS (Acquired Immune Deficiency Syndrome) (**Note:** New information currently becoming available—mechanism isn't completely understood.)	High-risk activities: Sexual activity with someone who is infected with AIDS and IV drug use. Transmitted through body fluids (semen, blood).

Table 13-1 (*continued*)

Symptoms	Results
Usually shows up 2–6 days after sexual contact. *For men*: pus dripping from penis or burning feeling while urinating; 10 percent have no symptoms. *For women*: slight vaginal discharge with burning but usually no symptoms at all.	Sterility in men and women. If a mother has gonorrhea when her baby is born, it must get medication or it may go blind. Arthritis, heart trouble, and general bad health. *For women*: one complication is an inflammation of the pelvic organs.
Painful blisters on genitals, sometimes on thighs and buttocks. They last 7–24 days. The sores will go away, but the disease will not. The sores can occur over and over again. Stress might be one reason why they recur.	*For women*: The chance of getting cancer of the cervix is higher, so women with herpes should have regular pap smears. Newborn babies can get herpes as they pass through the birth canal. Herpes can hurt the central nervous system and the baby could die.
The first sign is a sore or "chancre." It is very contagious and usually painless. *In men*: it is on the penis. *In women*: it is inside and around the vagina. Chancres may also show up on the mouth or breasts and cause swelling in the groin. They disappear in 3–6 weeks. **The second stage.** About 1–6 months later, people with syphilis get flu symptoms: they are tired and feverish; their joints and muscles hurt. They might get a painless rash on the palms of their hands or soles of their feet, swollen lymph nodes, and hair loss in patches. **The third stage** (the latent or silent stage). The disease travels all over the body for 1–20 years.	If the mother is pregnant and the baby gets infected, it can die or be seriously hurt. If the disease enters stage 3, it can be very serious: brain damage, heart and blood vessel disease, kidney disease, and possible death.
Fatigue, loss of appetite, extreme weight loss. Swollen lymph glands all over body. Night sweats. Skin infections that won't heal. Fever. Diarrhea.	Most AIDS victims die.

For Reflection
and Discussion

- The chapter stated that sexually transmitted diseases *are not selective*. What does that mean?

- What is gonorrhea? syphilis? herpes?

- Your friend says, "Only homosexuals get AIDS." How would you respond?

- How would you answer the question: What is the best method for preventing STD?

Chapter 14
Some
Touch Hurts

For though the will to do what is good is in me, the power to do it is not: the good thing I want to do, I never do; the evil thing I do not want—that is what I do.
—Romans 7:18–19

Touch can be warm and loving—a hug from that special friend or the warmth of a loving parent rubbing your back. Touch can also be painful and devastating. The fact is that *some touch hurts.*

As long as we have both the will and the power to do what is good and as long as we stay true to our values of respect of self and others, our touch will be that which heals, not that which hurts.

Touch Can Be Healing

When shared as a reflection of care and consideration for another, touch is one of the most powerful and pleasing experiences that humans can share. You can read in the Gospels about the healing power of Christ's touch. Just as Jesus healed with touch, so do we as human beings.

I am sure you can appreciate the special healing effects of the touch of a surgeon or the manipulation by a chiropractor. Such extreme examples of touch highlight the special power, the special gift, which one human can transmit to another simply by touch. But there are many more common-day examples of the healing power of touch.

You have probably seen the soothing, healing effect of touch as a mother quiets her upset infant simply by cuddling him or her. Or, perhaps you have experienced the comforting effect of a hug from a special friend at a time when you needed it. These are all examples of our human need for touch and the potentially powerful nurturing and healing force of healthy, loving touch.

Abusive and Hurtful Touch

Not all touching, however, is good or healing. Touch can be degrading and exploitive. Touch can violate a person's human rights and integrity. Touch which hurts, either physically or emotionally, is considered *abuse*.

Sometimes the abuse involves being touched in sexual ways. *Sexual abuse* is a touch which is unwanted, forced, and involves sexual contact.

Sexual Abuse

Sexual abuse is characterized by violence and force. The force or the power exerted can be physical, psychological, social, or emotional. Sexual abuse, therefore, involves an abuse of power and, as such, is a violation of the value of social justice.

Sexual abuse includes more than forced sexual intercourse (rape). All sexual contact between an adult and a minor, or between nonconsenting adults, is sexual abuse, even if it is limited to touches in the area of the genitals or breasts. Hurtful touch is imposed or forced on the other and is not how God means for us to use this gift.

Types of Sexual Abuse

There are two general forms of sexual abuse. The first has been termed *noncontact abuse*. Noncontact abuse refers to experiences such as encounters with *exhibitionists* (people revealing themselves sexually), or experiences of being approached to engage in sexual activity—but where no physical contact actually occurs, such as with an obscene telephone call.

The second form of sexual abuse is *contact abuse*. Contact abuse includes all behaviors that do involve sexual contact which is *forced and unwanted*—including fondling of breasts and genitals, intercourse, and oral and anal sex. While there are many forms of such contact abuse, three—rape, date rape, and incest—will be discussed in some detail.

134

Rape

Rape refers to forcing someone to have sex against his or her will. Rape, while most frequently happening to a woman, can happen to a man. Men have been known to rape other men or boys. Rape *is not* a love-making act. It is the *violent, hostile* invasion and domination of another.

Many people believe that rape happens only in dark alleys or parks. Some people believe that rape occurs only between a stranger and a victim. The sad reality is that:

- Half of all rapes happen at the victim's home.

- People are often raped by someone they know, someone they have met. This is known as "acquaintance rape."

There are other misunderstandings about rape. Some people feel that rape occurs because the woman asked for it. *Nothing could be more incorrect.* Rape is a violent, hostile act. No one wishes or asks for such abuse. Women or men who are raped, *do not ask* to be raped. Women and men who are raped *are not to be blamed and are not at fault!*

This last point is essential to remember. Too often, people who have been raped are treated as if they deserved it or as if it were their fault. A person who has been raped is a *victim*. As a victim, the sexual abuse is *never* their fault.

Date Rape

Rape occurs *anytime* a person forces someone to have sexual intercourse against his or her will. *Force* can come in a variety of forms. Certainly, holding a knife or gun to someone is force. But a person can be forced by means other than physical threat. A person who uses tricks to touch someone against his or her will (for example, by getting the person drunk) is a person using force to engage in sexual activity with this person. A person who threatens another by stating that if the person doesn't have sex they will spread rumors about them is using force to have sex with someone against his or her will. Even the person who threatens to break off the relationship or withdraw their love if their partner does not engage in sex is forcing another person to engage in sex against his or her will. Such coercion, such forced sex, is also *rape*.

Date rape, or acquaintance rape, happens when a friend or someone a person knows pressures him or her into having sex. As noted above, the pressure doesn't have to be physical,

135

although sometimes it is. Date rape is much more common then most of us wish to admit and it needs to be stopped.

Incest

Incest is sexual abuse that happens inside a family. The research would suggest that the abuser is most often a man—a father, stepfather, grandfather, uncle, big brother or cousin—but could be a woman, too. The victim of incest could be a boy or a girl.

Because of the power that an adult family member has over a child, many incest victims are ashamed of the abuse they experience but are afraid of telling another family member or outside adult. Children who are sexually abused within their family are:

- often threatened by the abuser not to tell anyone

- are convinced by the abuser that it is (was) the child's fault

- misinterpret the abuse as a sign of the abuser's love and, therefore, are afraid to say anything or to resist, for fear of losing the abuser's love

- feel too awful and devastated to talk about it

Sexual abuse, especially incest, leaves many scars—scars which may take years to heal. Even if incest happened only once and was a long time ago, it can take years for someone to recover from it.

More than anything else the victim of incest—the victims of all sexual abuse—must come to accept that *it is not their fault!*

The Scars of Hurtful Touch

The experience of sexual abuse leaves deep and extremely damaging scars. The *initial* effects (those occurring within two years of the termination of the abuse) have been reported to include reactions of fear, anxiety, depression, anger, hostility, and inappropriate sexual behavior. But the impact of sexual abuse is more extensive than the symptoms reported during the first two years following the abuse.

Research has found that there are *long term*, often lifelong effects of an experience of sexual abuse. Adults who have been victimized as children are likely to be depressed. They often show self-destructive behaviors (for example, attempting suicide) because they feel so poorly about themselves (poor self-esteem) and often feel that they are branded and rejected by others. Feeling unloved and unlovable, many of these victims seek escape from their pain through drug and alcohol use or even suicide.

Many victims of sexual abuse fail to demonstrate such extreme reactions. However, the research would suggest that many of these victims have difficulty trusting others and often show problems having healthy, normal sexual relationships.

Sexual abuse is an abuse which continues to hurt and damage well after the act itself has stopped. The short-term and long-term impact of sexual abuse highlights how essential it is for us to take steps to stop abuse when it is occurring and prevent abuse before it occurs.

An Ounce of Prevention Is Worth a Pound of Cure

You need to realize that you are not invincible. Abuse can happen to you. You need to begin to learn how to protect yourself. Some of the things you can begin to do in order to protect yourself are found in table 14–1.

Table 14–1
Know How to Protect Yourself

1. **Trust Your Feelings.** If you are feeling scared, confused, or just uncomfortable, there is probably a good reason.

2. **Remember That You Could Be at Risk.** Anyone can be a victim. It is easier to think about protecting yourself if you know that it could happen to you—not just to other people.

3. **Think about Situations That Could Be or Are Unsafe.** Avoid them, or make sure someone you trust is with you. Talk about it with someone you trust, too.

4. **Do Not Be Afraid to Ask for Help.** If you are in danger or afraid, it is smart to ask someone for help. It is *not* a sign of weakness. It is just common sense.

5. **Do Not Try to Handle Everything on Your Own.** If something has happened to you, or if you are afraid or confused, a counselor or another adult you trust can help you talk through you feelings.

6. **Use Common Sense Self-defense Rules.** (The ones you've always heard):

   • Do not walk alone at night.

   • Do not take rides from people you don't know very well.

   • Do not hitchhike.

   • And all the others. They make sense!

7. **Do Say What You Mean and What You Want.** If someone is pressuring you, you can say no! If someone touches you in a way that you do not like or that is confusing, you can tell them, or just leave and talk to someone about it. Do not let friends or anyone else talk you into doing something that seems scary or unsafe. Trust your feelings.

In addition to these specific suggestions, you need to understand and accept the fact that *anytime* a person is forced to engage in sexual activity against his or her will, it is *abuse.* Knowing the abuser (be that person a friend or a family member) does not excuse the act. Date rape is *rape* and must not be excused as simply something done because of passions or the heat of a moment.

Secondly, you need to begin to recognize who potential sexual abuse offenders might be and under what conditions you are at risk. A person who gives you a "power stare" (who stares hard and long trying to intimidate you) or a person who sits too close, even after you attempt to move back, may be signaling that this is a potentially high-risk situation. A friend or a family member who consistently "accidentally" brushes against you, or touches your breasts or genitals, or the family member or friend who greets you with a hug or a kiss which makes you feel uncomfortable, is signaling that this is a high–risk situation.

Finally, you need to develop an action plan on what steps to take in the event that someone tries to sexually abuse you. The first and perhaps most important step to take is to accept the fact that an experience with sexual abuse makes you a victim. Sexual abuse *is not your fault.* You are a *victim!* You have nothing to be embarrassed about. You have nothing to feel guilty about. You have the right, the absolute right, to have this stop. Next, if possible, you tell the abuser to stop. Move away from them. Tell them NO. Assert your right to resist this abuse. This is sometimes difficult and dangerous especially if the abuser is using physical force and threat. Needless to say, while it is important for you to firmly and assertively tell them to stop, you should not risk your life at that moment. The next step in your action plan is to report the incident of abuse. Reporting the abuse will not only help lower the probability of it happening to you again, but will help prevent that abuser from attempting it on another victim. You need to **tell** someone, especially someone you trust. **Keep telling** someone until you are believed and action is taken against the abuser.

What If It Happens to My Friend?

Sexual abuse can happen to you or to one of your friends. If a friend shares with you that they have experienced an incident or incidents of sexual abuse, as upset as you may be, you need to be able to affirm and care for your friend at that moment. You will need to support your friend and encourage him or her to seek help. To provide the support your friend needs, you should:

- Listen to the person in a calm and caring manner.

- Tell your friend that you do believe him or her.

- Tell him or her *not to blame himself or herself.*

- Be willing to go with him or her as your friend makes contact with an adult (a teacher, a doctor, a family friend or family member, or a professional) who can help with this situation.

You need to care for your friend who has been abused, but you must remember that caring for them demands that you report the incident. Keeping this a secret, while at first appearing like the easiest thing to do in order to avoid embarrassment or confrontation, is the wrong step for healing the hurt of the abuse. The abuse must be identified. The abuse must be reported. The abuse must be stopped and prevented from happening again. Stay with your friend as he or she begins this step of healing.

Touching as Love

With all the attention sometimes given to the harmful effects of touch and the many faces of abuse, you need to remind yourself that, like all gifts from God, the gift of touch is meant to be used positively. It is true that evil does exist. You need to learn how to trust your instincts about people and how to react to any attempts to impose unwanted and forced touch on you. But it is essential that you do not forget that human touch is good and necessary in healthy, caring relationships.

A touch of love is a beautiful reflection of the love of God. To touch with love is a miracle. Such touch can soothe a hurt or heal the pain of loneliness.

When you touch someone in ways that reflect your respect for that person and your loving concern, you can help them feel alive. Like Jesus, your touch doesn't have to be restricted to the touch of another's body. You can touch people at the level of their hearts. Touch them through an invitation to join you in sharing good experiences. Touch them by risking opening up and sharing of yourself.

When you touch—physically, psychologically, and spiritually—from an orientation of love and respect, you touch as God had intended. You touch with love.

For Reflection and Discussion

- Often people suggest that women who are raped are somehow at fault. *Nothing* could be more *incorrect!* How would you respond to somebody who believed that a woman was to blame for having been raped?

- What are the subtle forms of coercion that can go on during a date and result in *date rape?*

- Sexual abuse leaves deep and extremely damaging scars. What are some of the immediate and long-term effects of sexual abuse?

- How should you respond to a friend who has experienced or is currently experiencing sexual abuse?

Chapter 15
Being an Askable Parent (or Friend)

*I give thanks to my God every time I think of
you—which is constantly, in every prayer I
utter—rejoicing, as I plead on your behalf, at the way
you have all continually helped promote the gospel
from the very first day. I am sure of this much: that
he who has begun the good work in you will carry it
through to completion, right up to the day of Christ
Jesus.*
—Philippians 1:3–6

One of the primary reasons for this chapter is to help you
appreciate how tough it is to be a parent. For every question
that you ask your mom and dad, they have many more for
you. For every anxiety you feel about being a teen, your
parents have similar concerns and anxieties.

When they question you, it is often because they are afraid.
They are afraid that they might not be doing all that they
should. They may be afraid that they simply have missed the
mark. They may be concerned that they are not good parents.

Parenting is one of the few important roles that really is
learned "on the job." Yet, many parents expect themselves to
be totally and perfectly competent. So part of the reason for
this chapter is to help you begin to learn those parenting skills
which will make you a better communicating, Christian parent

and one who will continue to promote the gospel through the values you exhibit.

It is also hoped that as you consider what is demanded and required of a parent, you will begin to better understand and appreciate the struggles your parents experience.

There is another major goal for this chapter. It is hoped that you will share this chapter with your parents. In so doing, you might not only help them learn some new approaches and techniques but you might also open up a line of communication that will help you all grow.

Being Askable Requires Being Available

It is amazing how many parents panic at the thought of having parent-to-teen discussions on sex. As a result of this panic, many parents often make themselves either absent or unavailable to discuss these matters of concern.

Whether it be through the use of a phrase such as, "Go ask your mom (or dad)," or "Here, read this," or "You'll have that in school next year," parents often demonstrate their unwillingness or perhaps their inability to be available.

Why?

Parents' lack of availability may be a result of their own discomfort with the topic of sex and sexuality. Quite often, parents worry that they won't know the answer or know what to say.

It is certainly important that they have accurate information when they answer questions. However, parents need to accept the fact that they are not experts, nor do they have to be. They need to accept that it is okay to admit not having all the answers. It is even okay to admit being uncomfortable and nervous about a discussion on sexuality. But it is **not** okay to let these feelings be an excuse to avoid providing support and information to teens.

Anxious Yet Helpful

As teens, it helps if you can appreciate that your parents may be uncomfortable. Their own knowledge and expertise is less than perfect. However, your parents generally have a perspective, an insight, and set of experiences which you don't have and which might prove extremely helpful, if shared.

Much of what concerns you is knowledge and information that your parents might already possess. Concerns a boy might have over things such as nocturnal ejaculations (wet dreams), or uncontrollable erections are concerns his father also had. These concerns can be *shared*. Similarly, for the teen curious about the experience of pain and pleasure associated with intercourse, or the meaning of certain terms such as *French kissing*, there is a parent who was similarly curious at one time and who has the advantage of working through that curiosity.

There are clearly questions and concerns for which your parents do not have the information or the answer. But they do have their values, their insights, and their experiences which they can bring together with yours. Together, you may find the needed answers and support.

Parents need to appreciate that most often it is their willingness, interest, and availability to share with their teens that is more important than their expertise.

Helping your mom and dad (and yourself) accept that you don't have to be experts and that you don't have to be perfectly comfortable may help you resist running away from the issue. Becoming more available to one another enables communication, answers questions, and helps resolve problems.

Being Askable Means Being Approachable

Even when your parents are available for discussion and support, you may feel that they are unaskable. Sometimes this feeling comes from your own discomfort and anxiety. Sometimes it comes from the messages your parents send you.

Parents need to learn how to become askable. While perhaps desiring to be askable, many parents simply lack the knowledge and skills that are required of an *approachable* and thus, an *askable* parent.

Table 15–1 provides a list of characteristics typical of askable parents. These characteristics can be grouped in the following major categories:

- Askable parents respond with *presence*.

- Askable parents respond with *values*.

- Askable parents respond with *respect*.

Table 15–1
Characteristics of Askable Parents

- They really listen.

- They helps kids look for answers.

- They are honest.

- They take questions and feelings seriously.

- They talk about things that might be embarrassing or hard for teenagers to bring up.

- They are ready to talk on the spur of the moment without needing an appointment.

- They do not jump to conclusions when a teenager asks questions about sex.

- They answer the questions.

- They do not think they have to know everything.

Adapted from *Valuing Values: A Guide for Parents of Teens* by Rev. John E. Forliti (Dubuque, Iowa: BROWN Publishing-ROA Media, 1986).

Being Askable Requires Real Presence

Many parents approach a discussion of sexuality as if it were a one time event. They worry that this or that time may not be exactly the right time, for that special man-to-man or woman-to-woman talk. The right time to discuss sexuality is any time a teen asks! The difficulty is that often it is hard to know when the teen is asking.

Your parents may be waiting for you to come up and ask them to have a talk. Perhaps you have done this. Perhaps there have been questions which you felt were important and you simply said, "Mom and Dad, I'd like to talk." But most parents need to learn that teens most often ask in much more subtle ways.

The teen who shows a concern about taking showers in gym class, who seems embarrassed or especially curious about pictures or television shows with intimacy and romance, may be asking for some support. Since many of us fail to be as direct in asking questions or seeking support as we need to be, an askable parent will need to learn how to be more attentive, more **present** to the subtle questions which are asked.

To really be present and *to hear* the real questions being asked requires that we learn to be physically *and* psychologically present. One way of becoming psychologically present is through the use of a skill called *empathic or reflective listening.*

Empathic Listening

When you were young you were probably told to be a quiet, polite listener. You know: "Don't interrupt, just listen!" While it is important not to be judgmental and too interruptive, good listeners are not passive. If you want to truly understand what a person is saying, you have to see it or hear it from their point of view.

Empathic listening means listening as if *you* were the person speaking. Could you imagine how easy it would be to understand another person if you could think and feel exactly as they do as they talk to you? It would be like talking to yourself.

Empathic listening is kind of like crawling into the other person's way of being. That may sound like Star Trek, and mind-melding, but it really isn't that magical or mysterious. Research in psychology has demonstrated that there are a couple of skills you can use which actually help you to listen from the speaker's point of view. Obviously, as you learn to be more empathic, and listen from the speaker's point of view, you will more completely understand what is being said.

Think of the times you might have been upset about getting into an argument with a girlfriend or boyfriend. Your parents asked you what was wrong and you told them. They listened but then said, "Don't worry. There will be others." Your parents heard what you said but somehow they missed the real message. They missed the fact that this relationship was very special to you and that you are truly upset.

Could you imagine having your dad say, "I just lost my job," and feeling comforted by you or your mom when you say, "No big deal. There are other jobs." I doubt if he would think you really understood. However, if you were in your dad's shoes, or if your mom and dad really saw the world through your eyes, then all of a sudden losing a job or a special friend becomes more clearly a serious matter. This is listening empathically.

Empathic listening is an active, reflective form of listening. Reflective listening requires that you restate, or actively reflect to the speaker the message that they presented. This doesn't mean that you are a parrot or tape recorder. It does mean that you are paying such close attention to the speaker that you can stop them and reflect what you think they are trying to convey to you.

For example, your friend might say: "The dance is coming up and I really don't know who to ask. You know, so many choices." You may find yourself reflecting: "It sounds to me like you are unsure who to ask to the dance."

It may seem simple but by reflecting your received message back to the speaker you show them that you are really listening and that you want to receive the message accurately. Further, you may begin to find that as you pay attention and reflect the message you may even reflect messages that you received nonverbally. In this case, you may pick up not only **what** your friend said but *how* he or she said it.

In the same situation stated above, you may find that you reflect the following message: "It sounds to me that you are unsure who to ask to the dance. You sound a bit nervous." Often this reflection of the subtle messages you receive takes you and your friend to a deeper level of communication.

Because it is hard for many of us to express our feelings and concerns, a parent's ability (or, for that matter, your ability) to listen between the lines and go beyond the exact words of the message in order to tap into the meaning behind the words, is a very helpful process. In listening, you need to keep asking yourself questions such as: "What is he or she trying to say?" "What is the message he or she wants me to receive?" "If I were in his or her place, what would these words mean to me?"

Being Askable Requires Values

Parents can read every parenting book on the market, and you can practice being the best listener possible, but such skills are not enough. In addition to good communication skills, an *askable person* must value (prize) the other person and his or her need to be heard.

In discussing issues as important as sexuality, parents need to be able to not only provide answers, but to demonstrate through their own choices and decisions that they value these answers. Parents need to model the values that they wish their teens to acquire. It is not good enough to say one thing and do another.

In the area of sex and sexuality parents need to go beyond facts and figures. As Christian parents, they need to assist you in incorporating those values necessary to appropriately guide your use of these facts and figures. Parents need to reflect that they:

- Do rejoice in their own sexuality and that of their teen
- Do see sex as much more than genital activity
- Do view sexuality as an expression of Christ's loving relationship with us

Rejoice

As noted throughout this text, our sexuality is a gift from God. It is a gift to be enjoyed and one over which we need to take responsible stewardship.

For many unaskable parents, sex is something to be ashamed of or something to be hidden in the dark of the bedroom. Askable parents will value that sex is a gift which allows us to participate in the creative love of God, living in communion with Him through another. Askable parents rejoice in the awakening of their teen's sexuality because they know that such awakening is the invitation by God to experience oneness in relationship, in love.

More than Genital

The askable parent values sexuality as an invitation to relationship. Rather than narrowing the view of sexuality and restricting it to mean what goes on when one is physically stimulated, to the askable parent, sex is evidence of their teen's ability to share in a loving relationship. From such a relationship view of sex (rather than a genital view), askable parents approach the discussion of sex from a point of *do* rather than one of *don't.*

The askable parent feels free to encourage their teen to *share* and to *care* for another. Coming to share and experience the love of friendship is an essential part of being human and an active element of one's sexuality.

The askable parent values that the adolescent years are special years of sexuality. It is a period when the closeness and intimacy of a special friend can be experienced—through the sharing of dreams and disappointments and through caring in times of need.

Reflecting Christ's Love

With such a relationship view of sexuality, askable parents look forward to times of discussion with their teens. These times are not times of embarrassment but opportunities to share Christ's love. Askable parents value sexuality as an opportunity for *unselfish love*—the love which Christ so clearly modeled.

The askable parent understands that his or her teen needs a model of sexuality, a model for intimacy. Further, the askable parent welcomes the opportunity to provide Christ as this model. With Jesus as a model of intimacy, we can begin to understand that true intimacy is open and not secret or shameful. With Jesus as our model, we will appreciate that true intimacy is faithful to ourselves and to our partner. And with Jesus as our model, we will appreciate that our intimacy, our sexuality, is *other-oriented.* It is an unselfish desire to share in the love Christ has given to us.

With such values, parents are not only askable but desire being asked.

Being Askable Requires Respect

In addition to valuing a teen's sexuality, an askable parent also prizes and values his or her teen. Regardless of the many arguments you may have had with your parents over your hair, your grades, your room, and so forth, your parents value and prize you as a person. Thus, an askable parent doesn't make the teen feel strange or stupid or any other negative feeling because of the teen's concern about sexuality. Askable parents value their teens and respect them under all conditions.

While parents would not like to hear that their teen is involved in a sexual relationship, or that their child is pregnant, askable parents don't allow these conditions to reduce their respect and love for their teen. Knowing that they are loved and respected regardless of what has happened, or what they may have done, provides teens with the freedom to approach their parents under any and all situations. Such unconditional loving, valuing, and respecting is essential for the "Askable Parent."

Being Askable Requires You to Be Real

Perhaps more than anything, being askable requires that your parents step away from their *roles*—as teachers, disciplinarians, guides, and parents—and interact with you as real, vulnerable, genuine human beings.

The askable parent needs to appreciate that you are on a journey of development. It is a journey which you share with your parents. They need to convey to you that they, like you, are pilgrims and that they, like you, have decisions, concerns, and anxieties.

By being willing to open up and share his or her self, a parent becomes real, genuine, and most certainly **askable.**

For Reflection and Discussion

- Imagine that you are a parent of a thirteen year old. How would you feel discussing sexuality and values with your thirteen year old? What particular questions or issues may cause you discomfort?

- Make a list of five things you promise you will do as an "askable parent." (It may be interesting to save these and review them some years from now when you are parents.)

- What is empathic or active listening? What purpose does it serve? Could you demonstrate it?

- Sexuality is a gift from God. As such, we should rejoice in it. The chapter suggested that we need to understand that our sexuality is more than genital activity. Our sexuality is an expression of Christ's loving relationship with us. What does this mean?